GREAT AMERICAN HOMES

MANSIONS OF THE VIRGINIA GENTRY

BY HENRY WIENCEK
PHOTOGRAPHY BY PAUL ROCHELEAU

Oxmoor
House®

Great American Homes
was created and produced by
Rebus, Inc.
and published by Oxmoor House, Inc.

Rebus, Inc.
Publisher: Rodney Friedman
Editor: Charles L. Mee, Jr.
Senior Picture Editor: Mary Z. Jenkins
Picture Editor: Deborah Bull
Art Director: Ronald Gross
Managing Editor: Fredrica A. Harvey

Production: Paul Levin,
Giga Communications, Inc.

Author: Henry Wiencek, currently
editor of *The Smithsonian Guide to
Historic America,* is the author of
Plantations of the Old South (another of
the Great American Homes volumes).
He has also written histories of Japan,
Portugal, and Mexico.

Photographer: Paul Rocheleau is a
Massachusetts-based photographer
whose work has appeared in *Antiques,
Architectural Digest,* and *Americana*
magazines.

Consultant: R. Peter Mooz, Ph.D., now
director of the Mary Moody Northern
Foundation in Galveston, Texas, is the
former curator of the Wilton House
Museum in Richmond. A specialist in
American art, he has been museum
coordinator for the Winterthur
Program and has published articles on
American architecture and interiors in
several art and architecture magazines.

Published by Oxmoor House, Inc.
Book Division of Southern Progress Corporation
P.O. Box 2463
Birmingham, AL 35201

Library of Congress
Cataloging in Publication Data
Wiencek, Henry.
    Mansions of the Virginia gentry.

    (Great American homes)
    Includes index.
    1. Manors—Virginia. 2. Plantations—Virginia.
3. Architecture, Colonial—Virginia. 4. Classicism in
architecture—Virginia I. Title. II. Series
NA7613.V5W5 |728.8′3′09755 84-15499
ISBN 0-8487-0755-9

Cover: Monticello.

CONTENTS

FOREWORD 4

INTRODUCTION 6

CHAPTER 1
STRATFORD HALL: SQUIRES ON THE POTOMAC 16

PORTFOLIO
THE CULTURE OF THE EARTH 36

CHAPTER 2
SHIRLEY: THE STRENGTH OF TRADITION 46

PORTFOLIO
AN HANSOM CUPBOARD OF PLATE 60

CHAPTER 3
WILTON: THE ELEGANCE OF WOOD 72

PORTFOLIO
FURNISHING THE NEW LAND 84

CHAPTER 4
KENMORE: A NEW MODE OF DECORATION 94

PORTFOLIO
THE ART OF THE TABLE 108

CHAPTER 5
MONTICELLO: JEFFERSON'S MASTERPIECE 118

PORTFOLIO
DIVERSIONS OF A RENAISSANCE MAN 140

CHAPTER 6
MOUNT VERNON: WASHINGTON AT HOME 150

ACKNOWLEDGMENTS AND CREDITS 172

INDEX 173

FOREWORD

THE WEST PORTICO OF MONTICELLO

Of all Virginia's treasures, its Colonial architecture is its greatest—a rich heritage of gracefulness in brick and wood, artistry in plaster embellishments, fine furnishings, and beautiful gardens. But, above all, the great houses of Virginia are distinguished by an uncommon elegance, refined by a love of order and rationality. It is an ideal adopted from classical antiquity, as so many of the historic ideals of Virginia society are—an ideal that is embodied perfectly in the six houses shown in this book.

Stratford Hall stands on the Potomac River with commanding elegance. Its symmetry and steeply ascending staircase propel the eye to the center of the composition. Inside is a spectacular hall—the most important early paneled room in Virginia. This truly monumental space is ordered by a march of twenty Corinthian pilasters. A splendid room of fluted pilasters also greets the visitor at Wilton. Here, graceful arches and curved mantels add the dimension of movement, as does the staircase in the hall. Shirley boasts the ultimate in stairs: they fly upward from the floor of the great entry hall without visible support.

Betty Washington's Kenmore and George Washington's Mount Vernon are houses of new ideas. Kenmore's exterior is traditional but beyond the plain door is a surprise—the most spectacular plaster ceilings in the colonies. They are remarkable not only in the elaborateness of the decoration, but also because they are one of the earliest expressions of the neoclassical style in America. Mount Vernon is decorated with stucco, too. In certain rooms rococo designs are used, but the large dining room is ornamented in the Adam style. This room—perhaps the most accurate period room in America—was one of the earliest and most profoundly influential expressions of classical ornament in the new nation.

The spirit of inventive genius is the mark of Thomas Jefferson's Monticello, a masterpiece of neoclassical style that also announced the initial phase of Romanticism in America. Merely by choosing a mountaintop site, Jefferson proclaims the house a container of rational order in the midst of untamed nature.

The splendid photographs on these pages, and the carefully researched text, capture the spirit of these great houses, which are not only Virginia's proud heritage, but national treasures as well. Virginia's builders were among the chief founders of the republic, and these houses truly reveal the character of the men and women who created the nation.

R. PETER MOOZ
RICHMOND, VIRGINIA

INTRODUCTION

To the English settlers Virginia seemed another Eden. There were lush forests of oak and pine, abundant wildlife, and a congenial climate that made up for its fiercely hot and humid summer with a mild winter, an early and fragrant spring, and an autumn of surpassing beauty. In his history of the colony, published in 1705, Robert Beverley described the sensuous delights of the landscape: "Their eyes are ravished with the beauties of naked nature. Their ears are serenaded with the perpetual murmur of brooks....Their taste is regaled with the most delicious fruits....And then their smell is refreshed with an eternal fragrancy of flowers." The English traveler Andrew Burnaby, who visited Virginia in 1760, wondered at the "romantic and elegant" waterfalls, the rivers "winding majestically," the profusion of birds and game. By day he was enchanted by the "rich and vivid" colors of the butterflies, and at night by the fireflies: "The whole air seems to glow and be enlightened by them." All in all he said that "no country ever appeared with more elegance or beauty."

At the time of Burnaby's visit, eastern Virginia was no longer a wilderness, but the home of an aristocracy of tobacco planters who had developed a highly refined society. As Virginia's fortunes rose in the eighteenth century, so did scores of beautiful houses, perhaps the grandest collection of fine buildings in America. From the Potomac to the James, the colony resounded with what George Washington called "the music of hammers," until the riverbanks were dotted with the mansions of the Carters, Lees, Randolphs, and other first families. Some of

Mount Vernon, one of the finest Virginia mansions, was entirely designed by George Washington himself, with the aid of builder's stylebooks published in England. Nearly all the plantation houses in the colony were designed by their owners, who were inspired amateur architects.

7

the finest houses were designed by the planters themselves, for architecture was one of the pleasurable avocations of the well-to-do Virginian. Thomas Jefferson, an amateur architect of genius, said that building, or "putting up and pulling down," was his favorite amusement.

Until the early 1700s Virginia houses still retained the shapes of medieval architecture—towers, gables, and clustered chimneys gave the exterior a lively but somewhat disorganized look. Symmetry was haphazard: the front door might be more or less in the center of the facade; and when the family needed more space, they tacked on an addition or two without caring what the new wings did to the appearance of the house. Small casement windows shed a dim light on the interior, which often consisted of just two rooms per floor. The main door opened directly onto a large hall where the family ate, entertained, and sometimes slept within plaster, whitewashed walls, with exposed beams looming overhead. Few houses were built of brick or stone because of the Englishman's traditional preference for wood and the deep-rooted fear that houses of stone were unhealthy. As late as 1781 Thomas Jefferson decried the lingering prejudice against stone buildings in his *Notes on Virginia*. He tried to allay the ancient fears about the condensation that formed on stone or brick walls in humid weather and noted that stone and brick were more durable than wood and safer in a fire—novel ideas to the average eighteenth-century mind.

This 1825 painting shows a plantation as a self-contained unit, linked with the outside world by the river. The large white mansion on the hilltop, lording over the cluster of workshops and slave quarters, suggests the exalted status of the owner.

About 1720 Governor Spotswood finished building a new Governor's Palace in Williamsburg that provoked the admiration and envy of the colonials. It opened the eyes of the Virginians to a sweeping transformation in architecture that had occurred in England. The palace was designed in London in the English baroque style of Sir Christopher Wren. Gone was the vertical emphasis of towers and gables, and in its place English architecture had adopted the horizontal form, with the stress on aesthetically pleasing proportions and symmetrically arranged windows and doors. Once built a house could not easily be added to because an addition would ruin the carefully planned form. Brick was the favored material of the

Wren baroque style. A broad facade of various colors of rubbed and glazed bricks, combined with elements in contrasting white stone, created an "expansive richness," in the phrase of the art historian William Pierson.

The new style was gracious and had an aristocratic air of repose, befitting the new social and economic status of the planters. The orderliness of the Wren style required that the main house and its dependencies appear as a coherent, integral unit. In the eyes of the planters, this necessity became a distinct virtue: the previous clutter of wooden outhouses for the kitchen, schoolroom, stable, and workshops was reshaped into a neat arrangement of brick dependencies that formed a courtyard and enhanced the magnificence of the main house. The obvious contrast in size between the mansion and the outer buildings immediately proclaimed the superior nature of the master.

Shirley Plantation (Chapter Two), owned by the Carter family, has one of the most impressive arrangements of dependencies in Virginia. The kitchen, granary, laundry, and a storehouse form a forecourt on the landward side of the mansion.

In place of the common rooms of the seventeenth century, the new houses had separate bedrooms for privacy. In the second half of the eighteenth century, the first dining rooms appeared, reflecting the rise in wealth and the cultivation of fine social manners. Interior decoration underwent a change. Paneling with carved architectural elements such as pilasters and cornices lent a new richness to parlors and dining rooms. Thomas Lee's Stratford Hall (Chapter One) was among the first Virginia houses with carved paneling of this type; the parlor at Wilton (Chapter Three), which was built about twenty years later, is one of the last and most elaborate examples. Style aside, interiors became more comfortable, with better ventilation and more light. Beverley noticed the change: "The private buildings are...much improved.... They love to have large rooms, that they may be cool in summer. Of late they have made...their windows larger, and sashed with crystal glass."

Eighteenth-century American houses are often indiscriminately called Georgian, which is actually more useful as a chronological tag than a stylistic term. (There is even some chronological confusion: art historians sometimes limit the Georgian period to the reigns of the first three King Georges, 1714 to 1820, and sometimes expand it to include the fourth George, who reigned until 1830.) Several different architectural styles came and went during this era, flourishing first in England and arriving in America later. When the Wren baroque was the newest mode in America, it had already been supplanted in England by another style, Palladian. It was the style of ultrawealthy British lords, who built gargantuan country palaces that sometimes turned out to be uninhabitable. The style was inspired by the early-seventeenth-century work of the British architect Inigo Jones, who drew *his* inspiration from the Italian Andrea Palladio. Compared to British Palladian buildings, the American versions were country cousins; the colonists simply did not have the money to build on as magnificent a scale. Mount Airy, built in 1758 by John Tayloe, is one of the few Virginia houses that was totally Palladian. The influence of the style can be seen more in details of decoration and in isolated architectural elements. The imposing three-part window in the large dining room at Mount Vernon (Chapter Six) and the curved colonnades at the sides of the house are both Palladian features.

Huge hogsheads of tobacco are being stamped, weighed, and loaded onto ships in this cartouche from a map of Virginia made by Thomas Jefferson's father. A wealthy young planter sits smoking his pipe and awaiting a glass of wine.

In the second half of the eighteenth century, two Scottish architects, Robert and James Adam, wrought a complete change in interior design. They did away with heavy architectural ornaments and substituted "a beautiful variety of light mouldings, gracefully formed, delicately enriched and arranged with propriety and skill," in Robert Adam's own description. Light, graceful, and delicate are the perfect adjectives for the Adamesque motifs on the ceilings at Kenmore (Chapter Four) and Mount Vernon.

These new architectural forms signaled an aesthetic revolution in England and America. Houses were no longer built according to tradition, by craftsmen who followed the techniques of their fathers and grandfathers, but by architects who self-consciously worked within a style. Good taste became paramount: one had to select a fashionable design and the proper interior decorations to go with it. Since there were few professional architects in America until the nineteenth century, Americans relied on books to tell them what was fashionable and correct. English publishers issued numerous builder's guides with house plans and illustrations of decorative details. Abraham Swan's *British Architect* and *A Collection of Designs on Architecture*, James Gibbs's *Book of Architecture*, Batty Langley's *City and Country Builder's Treasury*, and Colin Campbell's *Vitruvius Brittanicus* were some of the guides Virginians consulted when they built.

Tobacco provided the wealth that fueled Virginia's prosperity after the colony's shaky start in the early 1600s. The men who founded Jamestown, the first permanent English settlement in the New World, nearly gave up and went home in the face of disease, Indian attacks, and starvation. Sir John Rolfe helped save the colony by marrying the Indian princess Pocahontas, thereby insuring peace with the Indians, and by cultivating tobacco. The Europeans looked on tobacco as one of the New World's greatest gifts to the Old. It was not smoked for pleasure at first, but for good health—to purge the body of "gross humors," open the pores, clear the body of obstructions, and cure gout, hangovers, and ague. Tobacco's greatest boon was that it made a lot of people rich.

Encouraged by the Crown, English settlers flocked to Virginia. They established farms along the four great rivers—the James, York, Rappahannock, and Potomac—that were deep enough for oceangoing ships. The planters soon discovered a problem with tobacco: after just a few years it exhausted the soil. They could plant corn and wheat in its place but had to obtain new land to plant their cash crop. A few men amassed enormous landholdings; but the prospects for an enterprising small farmer dimmed in the second half of the century. The Navigation Acts of the 1660s, designed to impose a British monopoly on the New World's most valuable commodities, limited Virginia's market to British traders. Prices fell, and only the large-scale planters could prosper with the reduced profit margin. By the end of the century, the best land was all taken. Virginia lost its allure for the small farmers and farm hands, who began emigrating from the colony. The well-to-do planters turned to the slave trade to solve their labor problem.

A British seaman made this watercolor view of the York River and the town of Gloucester. Four deep rivers—the York, Potomac, Rappahannock, and James—were the highways of Colonial Virginia; they carried oceangoing ships to the plantation's door.

For the prosperous planters with ample lands, Virginia was truly Eden, the fulfillment of the English Dream. Men whose grandfathers had been clerks, craftsmen, or shopkeepers in England leapfrogged the rigid British caste system and became gentry in America, with the tastes, attitudes, and customs of the British upper class. For one thing they took a personal interest in government, which in England was a pastime of the aristocracy. The roster of Virginia's governing bodies — the elected House of Burgesses and the appointed King's Council, which advised the governor—was virtually a social register. From 1680 to the Revolution, ninety-one men served on the King's Council; just twenty-three families contributed two thirds of the members.

Just as the English squire had his country estate, the Virginia aristocrat had his

The Governor's Palace in Williamsburg, designed in London in the style of Christopher Wren, inspired the colony's planters to erect fine mansions of their own.

plantation. In Virginia the plantation was the most important unit of society and commerce because there was no other. The colony had no cities to speak of because it had no need of them. Williamsburg was but a sleepy provincial capital with only a few year-round inhabitants. The plantation was a self-contained community that produced not only tobacco but meat, vegetables, fruit, and grains. Most were located by a river where ships arrived to carry tobacco to England and unload manufactured goods and luxuries. The plantation was more than just a large farm, it was a sizable community of the master's family, his employees, and slaves—often more than a hundred people in all. "When I reached his place I thought I was entering a rather large village," wrote a Frenchman of his visit to a plantation, "but later was told that all of it belonged to him."

For the slaves of the plantation, life was tedious and exhausting. In winter they hoed the stiff earth to make beds for planting. After the spring rains they slogged through the mud all day to make thousands of little hills of earth to receive the tobacco seedlings. They hauled and buried dung to fertilize the fields, pulled weeds, and plucked worms from the plants. A heavy rain might wash the seedlings from the hills, and the whole backbreaking process of making the mounds and planting the seedlings would have to be done again. They bent over thousands of times a day. When the tobacco had been cut down and dried, the slaves then worked at night to pack it into barrels, after working a full day in the fields. Their only payment was a small ration of corn and bacon. Not surprisingly the slaves were reluctant workers. One planter wrote that "the more particular we are in our charges and the fonder we show ourselves of anything the more careless will our slaves be." Planters' diaries suggest that no one—black or white—really cared to work very hard. White workmen tended to drink. Even the overseers had to be constantly watched and kept from the bottle. George Washington made a contract with some of his workers specifying the number of days they could be drunk.

The plantation system entered its heyday early in the eighteenth century. Virginians were beginning to savor the fruits of a stable economic system that every year produced increased wealth. Two marks of Virginia's progress were that it produced its first spectacularly wealthy planter— Robert "King" Carter, who owned over 330,000 acres, about 1,000 slaves, and had some 10,000 pounds in ready cash—and its first aesthete, William Byrd II. Byrd's grandfather had been a London goldsmith who married the daughter of a successful ship captain. Byrd's father inherited the captain's properties on the James River and made his fortune in trading rum, slaves, guns, and, in his own words, "anything else you may judge convenient for this country, fish excepted." William Byrd II, born in 1674, inherited substantial landholdings along the James and founded the city of Richmond on the site of his father's Indian trading post. He spent much of his life in London, where he moved in the highest social, literary, and scientific circles. He is famed for his diaries, written in a polished and sophisticated style, which provide a vivid picture of life in eighteenth-century Virginia.

William Byrd II, the self-proclaimed "ornament" of the colony, built a magnificent mansion on the James—Westover—with a handsome baroque entrance.

In 1726 Byrd wrote a letter to a friend in England describing his life as a plantation master as if it were a biblical idyll. "I have a large family of my own, and my doors are open to everybody, yet I have no bills to pay, and half a crown will rest undisturbed in my pocket for many moons together. Like one of the patriarchs, I have my flocks and my herds, my bondmen and my bondwomen, and every sort of trade amongst my own servants, so that I live in a kind of independence of everyone but Providence. [Although] this sort of life is without expense, yet it is attended by a great deal of trouble. I must take care to keep all my people to their duty, to set all the springs in motion, and to make everyone draw his equal share to carry the machine forward. But then 'tis an amusement in this silent country and a continual exercise of our patience and economy." The breezy style, the light-heartedness, and, particularly, the image of the plantation master as the man who must merely "set all the springs in motion" are all quintessential Byrd, but the letter also reflects the general contentment felt by Virginia's aristocrats. In the decades leading up to the Revolution, it seemed to the colony's upper class that life was virtually perfect and that only the edges needed polishing.

The plantation mansion was the center of aristocratic social life. The planter's isolation from his fellows made guests, even total strangers, a welcome sight. Travelers could call on any house and expect to be well fed and entertained. One foreigner wrote that it was "possible to travel through the whole country without money" except to pay ferry tolls. If a traveler offered to pay for his food at a house, "they are rather angry, asking whether one did not know the custom of the country."

Andrew Burnaby thought that the Virginians spent too much time socializing, a vice he attributed to the climate: "The climate and external appearance of the country conspire to make them indolent, easy, and good-natured: extremely fond of society, and much given to convivial pleasures." Indeed the Virginians were past masters of the convivial pleasures. They delighted in dining, dancing, drinking, gambling, fox hunting, and horse racing. So headlong did they throw themselves into the pursuit of their pleasures that they gained a reputation in the other colonies for outright decadence. Philip Vickers Fithian, a young Princeton man who came to Virginia in 1773 to tutor the Carter children at Nomini Hall, asked God to preserve him from the corruptions of the colony. "And I hope in the Kind-

Virginians avidly played all sorts of games and gambled recklessly at cards. "Burn me, if I pay anything more for such sport," wrote one disgusted planter in his diary. Benjamin Henry Latrobe sketched this scene of billiards players in a tavern.

ness of him who was my Fathers God, & has been the Guide of my Youth, that he will save me from being corrupted, or carried away with the Vices which prevail in that Country." Fithian kept a diary where he recorded the busy round of house parties, dances, and races the Carters attended. A rather dour Presbyterian,

Fithian was appalled at all the drinking and the passion for dancing. Fithian himself didn't dance, and at one party he got into an argument with a drunken Lee who asked why he bothered to come to the party if he wasn't going to take his turn on the floor. Later he wrote in his diary: "They will dance or die!"

The planters delighted in fox hunting—the preferred sport of the English aristocracy. George Washington, an expert horseman, was a particular devotee of the hunt. In this painting one man has been unhorsed leaping a fence.

House parties usually lasted several days and nights. The host decorated his entrance hall with potted orange trees, put candles over the doors, and brought mirrors down from the bedrooms to reflect the candlelight onto the dance floor. The servants set the tables with symmetrical arrangements of food and crescents of glasses. One room was reserved as a men's drinking room, another was set up for cards. The day's entertainment would include boat races on the river, or horse races. The dancing and drinking went on into the small hours of the morning, if it stopped at all. The guests stayed the night on the floor, dormitory style, with the men in one room and the women in another, sleeping on mattresses. Everyone would be up for breakfast at eight the next day, relax with a morning harpsichord performance by the ladies of the house, and then begin the drinking and dancing again.

The idyll lasted until the Revolution. The break with Britain, which Virginians so avidly fought for, brought their way of life to a close. The tobacco trade collapsed, and widespread economic depression in the early nineteenth century cost many Virginians their land. Logically Virginians should have been the last to rebel against Great Britain. Families such as the Lees had grown rich under the Crown, yet the Lees were among the first to cry for independence. In the words of the historian Daniel Boorstin, the Revolution was "the suicide of the Virginia aristocracy." Based as it was, on slavery, the system could not have endured; but the Virginians of course did not see it that way. Some of them saw in their way of life the re-creation of the ancient Roman nobility: the plantation was but another version of the villa on the hilltop. Others, such as Byrd, pictured themselves as biblical patriarchs, living peacefully under their own vines and fig trees—a line from the Old Testament that George Washington was fond of quoting. They discovered that in the new world they made by revolution there would be little time remaining for their pastoral visions.

1

STRATFORD HALL

SQUIRES ON THE POTOMAC

Stratford Hall is a formidable house. Its broad brick facade and massive chimneys stand with lordly pride atop a bluff overlooking the Potomac. With two wings connected in the center, the ground plan of the house forms a blunt and sturdy H. A stairway thrusts itself from the front of the house more as a challenge to the visitor than a welcome—ascend these stairs if you dare. Its formal rooms are on the second floor, an architectural device calculated "to add to the majesty of the whole aspect," according to the British builder's guide that may have inspired Stratford. The total effect is of a fortress, a fortress of power and privilege; but this baronial mansion was the birthplace of five of the colony's most dedicated revolutionaries, the Lee brothers.

John Adams referred to the Lees as "this band of brothers, intrepid and unchangeable, who like the Greeks at Thermopylae, stood in the gap, in defense of their country, from the first glimmering of the Revolution on the horizon." William and Arthur Lee were both diplomats in Europe, where Arthur helped persuade the French to send aid to George Washington's beleaguered army. Thomas served on Virginia's Committee of Safety, the revolutionary government; and Francis sat in the Continental Congress. But it may have been Richard Henry Lee who contributed the most to the cause. Before the war he helped form the committees of correspon-

---

Opposite: An alley bordered by tulip poplars leads to Stratford Hall, built about 1730 by Thomas Lee on a bluff overlooking the Potomac. Five of Lee's sons became leaders of the Revolution, and in 1807 Robert E. Lee was born at Stratford to Ann Carter and Light-Horse Harry Lee.

Overleaf: Glazed bricks on the first floor and borders of rubbed bricks on the second help to lighten the imposing facade of Stratford. The stairway ascends to the Great Hall on the second floor. The door was kept open during parties so that guests could stroll on the lawn and watch horse races.

dence that kept the distant colonies in touch with each other. In the Continental Congress it was he who introduced the resolution calling for independence from Britain. He and Francis were the only two brothers to sign the Declaration of Independence. All of them were unafraid to sever the links with Britain that had brought their family wealth and prestige.

Stratford was built about 1730 by Thomas Lee, the father of the Lee brothers, who was one of the most prominent planters in Virginia. As a young man Lee had acted as the land agent for the wealthy Fairfax family, the British owners of some five million acres of prime Virginia land. He rode throughout the colony to survey the Fairfax property, issue land grants to farmers, and collect the rents. He had a keen eye for farmland and purchased one of the most beautiful spots in Virginia, the Cliffs, a tract of about 1,400 acres along the Potomac where the riverbank rises steeply from the water. From this modest beginning Lee amassed an empire of some thirty thousand acres.

Thomas Lee (1690–1750), Stratford's builder, amassed a fortune dealing in tobacco and land. He owned about thirty thousand acres of prime Virginia land.

About a mile from the edge of the precipice he built Stratford and four dependencies, which housed the kitchen, workshops, storage rooms, and perhaps a school for his children. Lee landscaped the grounds of the mansion with typically British elegance and formality. He laid out a garden of box hedges and planted myrtle and dogwood for shade. But there was a touch of the exotic as well: orange trees, figs, pomegranates, and weeping willows, which were a novelty in America. In fact Thomas Lee was one of the first Americans to plant weeping willows.

After the aloofness of Stratford's exterior, the interior comes as a surprise: the rooms are gracious and warm, even intimate. The ground floor includes five bedrooms for the family and guests, rooms for the housekeepers, and a counting room where Lee kept his records and met with the ship captains who carried his tobacco to England. A narrow interior stairway leads from the ground floor to the second floor, where each wing of Stratford's H holds four rooms. The west wing includes two small rooms where guests left their overcoats and riding boots and sat briefly to refresh themselves before entering the more formal rooms; a parlor where the Lee family gathered for tea, drinks, or a game of cards; and a library. The dining room, in the east wing, is a modest room with simple paneling on the fireplace wall and wainscot surrounding the rest of the room. The bedroom on the southeastern corner—the sunniest spot in the house—is known as the Mother's Room. It was in this room that Hannah Ludwell Lee gave birth to the "band of brothers."

The Great Hall, "for feasts and other jollities," links the two wings and forms the crossbar of the H. Lee designed the hall to echo the grandeur of the exterior. Twenty-nine feet square, with a ceiling almost eighteen feet high, it was one of the largest private rooms of its day in Virginia. Paneling surrounds the room. Pilasters in the Corinthian style flank each door and window, and an entablature runs around the top of the paneling, lending an impressive architectural quality to the hall.

From the Great Hall the second-story location of the formal rooms works to its greatest advantage. Window seats on the southern side of the hall look out onto the lawn and groves of poplars, and on the northern side over rolling meadows to the wide Potomac. From this height the eye dominates the landscape, and one feels the sensation of lording over the land that produces in such abundance, and over the river that carries the world's commerce to one's door.

Feelings such as these must have stirred in the breast of Thomas Lee when he stood in this room. He was one of America's early visionaries, foreseeing the westward expansion of settlement at a time when many of his peers were content with piling up fortunes along the coast. In 1744 he journeyed from Stratford to Lancaster, Pennsylvania, to meet with the chiefs of the Iroquois and negotiate a vast land acquisition for Great Britain: territory that would become the future states of Kentucky, Ohio, Indiana, Illinois, Wisconsin, Michigan, and part of Minnesota— all for about four hundred pounds in cash and trinkets. With the approval of Great Britain, Lee and several other wealthy Virginians formed the Ohio Company to settle the Ohio Valley, which brought the British in direct conflict with French claims and set the stage for the French and Indian War.

In a portrait that hangs in the Great Hall, Lee wears the raiment of a man who had reached the pinnacle of Colonial success—the aristocrat's flowing wig and the scarlet robes of the King's Council. Before his death in 1750, he became the head of

---

Overleaf: The Great Hall was one of the largest rooms in eighteenth-century Virginia. A carved cornice and Corinthian pilasters surround the hall, which is almost eighteen feet high and is twenty-nine feet square. On the right a Chippendale sofa and chairs are arranged with a Queen Anne tea table.

the council, and in his letters he grandly signed himself "President of Virginia."

Thomas Lee's oldest son, Philip Ludwell Lee, inherited Stratford at the age of twenty-four. He lived lavishly, giving parties, fox hunting, and breeding racehorses. Richard Henry Lee lived a bachelor's life with Philip at Stratford in the 1750s. They shared a devotion to the hunt and to fine wines and food (Richard Henry eventually developed gout). While he was leading the luxurious life of a wealthy young aristocrat, Richard Henry was at the same time reading the radical political writings of John Locke, steeping himself in the philosophy of revolution. Under the same roof where Thomas Lee had planned the Treaty of Lancaster, by which he handed over millions of American acres to Britain, Richard Henry Lee read his Locke and contemplated a break with Britain. The pattern of a Lee son undoing the work of the father was one that would repeat itself on an equally grand scale in the next century.

Stratford was the scene of numerous parties during Philip Lee's tenure. He liked to give parties at Stratford's boat landing, with the guests and musicians on gaily lit barges anchored in the river. He organized horse races to entertain the guests and to show off his champion Thoroughbred, Dotterel—the second-fastest horse in England when Philip purchased him to start a stud farm at Stratford. During dances in the Great Hall, Philip would lead his guests up a narrow stairway through the attic to the chimneys on the roof. Each cluster of four chimneys was surrounded by a balustrade, forming pleasant pavilions where the guests could refresh themselves with a breath of cool Potomac air. According to family tradition Philip built a promenade linking the two clusters of chimneys, where guests danced under the stars to a band playing in one of the pavilions.

A brief account of a party at Stratford has survived in the diary of Philip Vickers Fithian: "About six in the evening the chariot returned with Bob, Miss Prissy & Nancy from the dance at Stratford," he recorded on January 8, 1774; "they brought news as follows: Miss Prissy told us, that they had an elegant dance on the

Opposite: An archway connects the dining room with a sitting room, where a full-length portrait of Queen Caroline of England hangs on the wall. She made Thomas Lee a gift of three hundred pounds after convicts, whom Lee had sentenced to prison when he was justice of the peace, escaped and burned down his first house.

Overleaf: In the parlor rococo candlesticks fashioned by the English smith John Case stand at a mahogany Chippendale gaming table, made in New York about 1765. The Hepplewhite desk-and-bookcase, mahogany with satinwood inlay, once belonged to Robert E. Lee. It was made in Salem in the 1790s.

whole...that Mr. Christian the master [the children's dancing instructor] danced several minuets, prodigiously beautiful; that Captain Grigg danced a minuet with her; that he hobbled most dolefully, & that the whole assembly laughed!"

Ten days later Fithian went to the home of another Lee for a party, which Fithian described in detail. Though this affair took place at the home of Richard Lee, the celebrations must have been similar to those Philip often hosted at Stratford.

"I was introduced," Fithian wrote, "into a small room where a number of gentlemen were playing cards to lay off my boots, riding-coat, etc....About seven the ladies and gentlemen begun to dance in the ballroom—first minuets one round; second giggs; third reels, and last of all country dances....But all did not join in the dance for there were parties in rooms made up, some at cards; some drinking for pleasure; some toasting the Sons of America [he probably meant the Sons of Liberty]; some singing 'Liberty Songs' as they called them, in which six, eight, ten or more would put their heads together and roar."

Ann Carter Lee rocked her infant son Robert E. Lee to sleep in this maple cradle. It was fashioned in the style of Southern cabinetmakers just a few years before Lee was born, on January 19, 1807.

One reveler who may not have joined in the raucous chorus of Liberty Songs was Philip, the only one of the Lee brothers not to take a public stand on independence. Since he sat on the King's Council, he was, in all likelihood, a Loyalist. He died in 1775 before the start of the Revolution, thus preserving the Lee family from an embarrassing public feud. His wife remarried, and Stratford was left to Philip's daughter Matilda, then just a teenager, but already possessed of the musical talent, fine looks, and gaiety that would earn her the nickname "the divine Matilda."

She and her sister, Flora, passed the war years quietly, giving shelter to relatives from more dangerous areas. In 1781 the Revolution burst upon Matilda in the

The sunny bedroom on the first floor was where Hannah Lee gave birth to the "intrepid band" of Lee brothers. Two generations later Robert E. Lee was born in this room. The fabric decorating the bed is a reproduction of a toile de Jouy with a motif of America paying homage to France.

person of her cousin General Harry Lee, the dashing twenty-six-year-old cavalry hero known to friend and foe as Light-Horse Harry. Tall, deeply tanned from his campaigns in the south, and full of battle lore and anecdotes about General Washington and the marquis de Lafayette, Harry charmed Matilda and won her hand. They were married in the Great Hall in the spring of 1782. Richard Henry Lee gave away the bride, and George Washington sent a supply of Madeira for the reception.

Stratford reached a peak of glamor with the handsome young couple as master and mistress, but the idyll was tragically brief. After bearing four children Matilda died in 1790, at the age of twenty-six. Harry found some relief in politics. He was elected governor in 1791 and while in Richmond met Ann Hill Carter of Shirley Plantation (Chapter Two), who became his second wife in 1793. After Harry's term in office ended, the couple went to live at Stratford, where signs of the master's neglect were already beginning to show.

Harry Lee the war hero was not cut out to be Harry Lee the plantation master — dogged, day-to-day industriousness was not his style. The ex-cavalry commander preferred the quick strike and speculated rashly in land and currency schemes in the hope of reaping an instant fortune. His investments ended disastrously. He was forced to sell parcels of the old Lee property to meet his debts and to support a growing family. On January 19, 1807, Ann gave birth to their fifth child, Robert E. Lee, in an atmosphere of gathering gloom. Harry Lee chained the doors of Stratford shut to keep out the creditors. Two years later the sheriff came to take him to debtor's prison.

Robert E. Lee spent the first four years of his life at Stratford. For a playground he had the meadows, groves, and gardens that Thomas Lee had carefully laid out some seventy years before. The willows, oaks, beeches, and sugar maples were in their lofty maturity, but the paths of the formal garden were overgrown and forlorn. After Harry Lee's release from prison, the family moved its few remaining possessions to a small house in Alexandria, leaving Stratford to one of Harry Lee's sons by his first wife. In 1813 Harry went into self-imposed exile. He had been severely beaten in Baltimore as he was trying to defend a Federalist newspaper from destruction by a mob. Badly mutilated, and suffering from painful internal injuries, he went to

The nursery, which is connected to the master bedroom by two doorways, contains children's furniture, a miniature tea set, a wooden toy horse on wheels, and two beds. The children slept in the arched tester camp bed, and the smaller canopied bed was for a doll.

Light-Horse Harry Lee, the great cavalry hero of the Revolution, became master of Stratford in 1782 when he married his cousin Matilda, who had inherited the house from her father.

Barbados to seek relief in the warmer climate and died five years later without seeing his family again.

In the years after the Revolution, Harry Lee had been one of the champions in the cause of a strong union. In public debate he took on Patrick Henry and others who advocated the right of the states to retain sovereign power. It fell to his son to lead the forces of disunion. Robert E. Lee was personally opposed to secession, but when the time came to choose between the North and the South he knew that he could not take up arms against his own people. Once again a Stratford Lee felt compelled to cut bonds that his father had helped to forge.

One Christmas in the midst of the Civil War, after Lee had lost his home, Arlington, his thoughts went back to Stratford, which remained a happy place in his memory, linked with his warm recollections of his father. He wrote to his wife, "I wish I could purchase Stratford. That is the only other place I could go to, now accessible to us, that would inspire me with feelings of pleasure and local love."

The Lees conducted the business of the plantation in the counting room. A Windsor comb-back chair and Chippendale armchair flank a pine-and-maple tavern table. The letterpress in the background was used to keep documents in order. In this unheated room the clerk would have put his feet on the warmer under the table.

Overleaf: Stratford's kitchen is in a building separate from the house. The enormous oven, twelve feet wide, six feet high, and five feet deep, could roast a whole ox. The spit clock fastened to the wall automatically turned the roasting spit, powered by the weight hanging from a pulley.

THE CULTURE OF
THE EARTH

The plantation masters of Virginia considered a fine garden to be the indispensable ornament of a well-designed mansion. Men with sufficient means to pursue the art often sent plants from the New World back to England in exchange for cultivated varieties, which they laid out in imitation of English gardens: geometric designs, clipped boxwood hedges, and elaborate topiary. The garden at Agecroft Hall (pages 40–41), a fifteenth-century English manor house reconstructed in Richmond, offers a look at the gardening tradition shared by the colony and the mother country.

By the end of the eighteenth century, gardening styles in England had gradually evolved into a more casual naturalism that was widely copied here. During this period Virginia's premier statesmen were among her finest gardeners. George Mason, who wrote the Virginia Declaration of Rights and helped draft the Constitution, derived continued pleasure from the earlier style and planted formal gardens called parterres, outlined in boxwoods (pages 38–39). Washington chose a less formal scheme for the gardens at Mount Vernon (Chapter Six), still well ordered, but with curving walks and areas he called "Wildernesses." Jefferson, the most radical of the three, planted no boxwoods at all at Monticello (Chapter Five). He made his flower beds oval, his walks serpentine, and the views from his prospects varied and spectacular. Jefferson once wrote to the artist Charles Willson Peale, "No occupation is so delightful to me as the culture of the earth and no culture comparable to that of the garden."

Mount Vernon. *A crepe myrtle blooms at the entrance to Washington's Upper Garden, described by the architect Benjamin Latrobe as "a neat flower garden laid out in squares and boxed with precision." Records indicate that this garden contained vegetables and boxwood hedges in addition to flower beds.*

Gunston Hall. *Looking south across flowering quince and the carefully clipped boxwoods of the lower parterre, the view from Gunston Hall extends over a deer park to the Potomac River. George Mason's formal arrangement*

of his garden, fashionable in Virginia in the seventeenth and early eighteenth centuries, was somewhat outmoded in his time, having been replaced by a more naturalistic style.

Agecroft Hall. *White candytufts and parrot tulips bloom in spring in the formal garden at Agecroft; in summer they are replaced by pink geraniums. The garden's centerpiece is an astrolabe—a medieval instrument that was used to determine the height of the sun.*

The herb garden at Agecroft is laid out in intricate designs called knots: plantings of lavender, germander, barberry, and hyssop alternate with colored pebbles. The ground cover in the bed against the brick wall bears the name "lamb's ear" and is soft to the touch.

Virginia House. *Yellow tulips and pink and white hyacinths line the path from the back of this house, which was reconstructed in Richmond from the stones of an English monastery. The west wing of Virginia House is a reproduction of part of Sulgrave Manor, the home of Washington's ancestors in England.*

The view from the garden overlook shows a variety of trees—cedar of Lebanon, Japanese maple, flowering dogwood, and Southern red oak—on a hill that slopes gently to the James River. A path leads to two lower gardens, one that is planted with azaleas and the other with water lilies and lotuses.

Monticello. *Bearing melons and broccoli late into the fall, Jefferson's vegetable garden extends nearly one thousand feet along the south slope of the mountaintop, and the view sweeps to the horizon. His decision to build his*

house on a mountain—he was the first American to do so—produced endless difficulties in maintaining a water supply for the house and gardens, but ensured beautiful prospects in every direction.

2
SHIRLEY

THE STRENGTH OF TRADITION

In the same decade when Thomas Lee was building his baronial house at Stratford, John Carter and his wife, Elizabeth, were building an entirely different kind of house on the north bank of the James River, at the old Shirley plantation. Though John was the eldest son of "King" Carter, unlike Thomas Lee he felt no need to proclaim his personal magnificence with a daunting mansion. Where Stratford is massive and aloof, Shirley is tall, graceful, and welcoming—a two-story brick house topped by a carved pineapple that, in the eighteenth century, symbolized hospitality.

John Carter started work on the house sometime after he came to Shirley Plantation from his family seat at Corotoman and married Elizabeth Hill in October 1723. The Hill family had been raising tobacco on Shirley Plantation's seven hundred acres since at least 1655 and occupied a large mansion that John left standing when he constructed Shirley. The old Hill house, as it came to be called, was not demolished until 1868.

John Carter posed for this oil portrait in the London studio of Godfrey Kneller. Carter married Elizabeth Hill in 1723 and began building Shirley about ten years later.

A portrait in the parlor shows John as a handsome young man, with a smooth round face, a wide mouth, and a slightly haughty air about him that he picked up in the salons of London, where his father had sent him to study law and prepare

---

Built in the 1730s by John Carter, Shirley received its grand Palladian portico about one hundred years later, when Hill Carter was master. The plantation that surrounds the mansion has been in the Hill and Carter families for ten generations, since the middle of the seventeenth century.

himself for the duties of a planter and a Virginia aristocrat. When John came home in 1722, King Carter used his influence and purse to install his son in no less a post than secretary of Virginia. This lifetime appointment, purchased for £1,500 in cash, brought John the princely annual salary of 122,000 pounds of tobacco, plus an office at Williamsburg. His father also arranged for John to be appointed to the King's Council.

Funeral hatchments—painted coats of arms—were displayed in the house of the deceased. This rare, early-eighteenth-century hatchment memorializes one of the Hill family.

Given John Carter's lofty position in the colony, it is a little surprising that the house he built was not larger. He designed a compact, intimate house with only four rooms on the first floor. He obviously did not intend to impress his visitors with the size of his house—he had a more clever architectural gesture in mind. The stairway in the entrance hall ascends from the ground floor to the attic in a graceful, squared-off spiral, sweeping aloft without any apparent support. Unseen stringers secure the stairway to the walls; but a visitor standing at the foot of the stairs would scratch his head and wonder how it was done. The "flying" stairway was, in one way, John Carter's lighthearted signature on his house: it displays an imaginative flair not often found in the mansions of his peers. On a practical level the unusual design created some much needed open space in the entrance hall—a room where Virginia parties often took place—but even so the room could accommodate only a small group of dancers for a minuet. The more energetic reels and jigs would have been impossible in that relatively confined hall—the Carters probably held their dances outdoor by the river.

Little is known of the private life of John and Elizabeth Carter. They were close friends of their neighbor William Byrd II of Westover, who referred to Elizabeth as "a good-humoured little fairy" in famous diaries. Byrd's son, William Byrd III, married the Carters' daughter, Elizabeth; but the match was not a happy one.

Opposite: Concealed iron supports, not discovered until recent renovation work, anchor the "flying" section of Shirley's famed staircase to the wall. The hanging cast-iron lamp is an English piece made about 1790. A portrait of King Carter, father of the builder, looks down on the entrance hall.

Overleaf: Family furniture and silver from the eighteenth century furnish Shirley's dining room. Charles Carter purchased the mahogany table, the armchairs, and the mirror in the 1770s when he renovated the mansion. The silver fruit bowl on the table bears the portrait of Nestor, Carter's champion racehorse.

Elizabeth suspected her husband of philandering and, one day when he was out, tried to search his chest of drawers for incriminating letters. The chest toppled over and killed her.

Letters indicate that John Carter shared the popular taste for gambling on the horses and drinking fine wines. In a letter to a London merchant, he wrote, "Send me every year four pipes of the best wine the island [Madeira] produces [because I intend] to break myself of the habit I long had of drinking claret. And pray order them particularly to let my wines be white, for I do not like the tinctured or deep colored." His half brother Landon, who was something of a blue-nose, characterized John as frivolous in his journals; but the records that do survive show that John took his duties as a plantation master and a government official seriously. Even his gambling he conducted with businesslike order.

A graceful broken pediment, with scrolls terminating in rosettes, decorates a dining room doorway. In the eighteenth century a carved pineapple was a symbol of hospitality and an apt motif for the dining room of a generous host.

When John Carter died, in 1742 at the age of forty-six, he left Shirley to his son Charles with the proviso that Elizabeth be allowed to live there for the rest of her life. Elizabeth married a widower named Bowler Cocke, who was a good plantation master—like many other progressive Virginia farmers, he abandoned tobacco and planted wheat instead—but a poor caretaker of the mansion itself. An English traveler passed by Shirley in 1770 and found it run down: "This is indeed a charming place; the buildings are of brick, large, convenient, and expensive, but now falling to decay.... The present proprietor has a most opulent fortune and possesses such a variety of seats, in situations so exceedingly delightful, that he overlooks this sweet one of Shirley, and suffers it to fall to ruin."

Charles set things to right at Shirley soon after the death of his mother and her husband in 1771. He moved in himself and hired builders to adorn the walls of the downstairs rooms with a lavish expanse of paneling, including dramatic broken pediments over the doorways and a detailed carving of oak leaves and acorns over the fireplace in the parlor. Atop the doorway of the dining room, Charles placed a carved pineapple, saying, in a sense, that in this room the visitor would find the hospitality promised by the pineapple on the roof. To give his hospitality the appropriate glitter, he ordered a generous amount of elegant silver tableware from London—platters, bowls, tea and coffee services, candlesticks, punch strainers, and the whole gamut of knives, forks, and spoons required for proper dining in the eighteenth century. He never tired of proclaiming his eagerness to be a good host, and placed the pineapple symbol atop his tea service. Altogether he owned nearly sixty items of silver. In honor of his champion racehorse, Nestor, he ordered a silver punch bowl with a full-length portrait of Nestor engraved on it. Whenever the horse won Carter ordered up champagne, and Nestor slurped a victory drink from his very own bowl.

No descriptions of Charles Carter's entertainments have survived; but as a planter of wealth and importance, he must have been a frequent host. One of his guests in the 1790s was Light-Horse Harry Lee, then governor of Virginia. After the death of his first wife, Lee

In the 1770s Charles Carter's woodcarver fashioned an intricate band of oak leaves and acorns for the parlor mantel. According to family tradition most of the acorns have been pried off by generations of Carter boys testing their jackknives.

courted Charles' daughter Ann and finally won her hand after promising Carter that he would not sail off to France to fight in the revolution there. The wedding took place in the parlor at Shirley in June 1793, with just a few guests in attendance because it was Harry Lee's second marriage. The couple moved to Stratford, but Lee's financial troubles led Ann to take refuge with her children, including the young Robert E. Lee, at Shirley.

Charles Carter died at the age of seventy-four, in 1806. His grandson Hill Carter took over Shirley several years later. As a teenage midshipman in the Navy, Hill had seen action in the War of 1812. With a cutless clenched in his teeth, he led a boarding

---

Overleaf: The paneling of the parlor may have been modeled on designs in a British builder's guide by Abraham Swan. The sofas, purchased by Charles Carter, are attributed to Peter Scott of Williamsburg. The oil portrait by John Wollaston over the mantel depicts Elizabeth Hill Carter, the builder's wife.

party that captured a British sloop off Florida and was awarded a ceremonial sword by Congress for his bravery. The young war hero took to plantation life with pleasure. He made Shirley's acres the most productive in the region by experimenting with different kinds of fertilizer; and he was a diligent caretaker of the mansion. He built porticoes around the land and river entrances to the house—imposing Palladian-style porches with two tiers and pediments on top. His porticoes added a monumentality to the house, a touch of the splendid, without making the mansion overbearing. When Hill Carter made these additions, in 1831, the Palladian style had been out of fashion for several decades. In fact Shirley had become almost a museum of eighteenth-century style amid Greek Revival and Victorian Virginia.

In 1854 ex-president John Tyler and his wife, Julia, stopped at Shirley and were amazed at the extremely conservative taste of the Carters: "Shirley is indeed a fine old place," Mrs. Tyler wrote in a gossipy and not entirely grammatical letter to her mother, "but if it were mine I should arrange it so differently. I should at least have the parlor in better taste and in conformity with modern fashion. Old & fine portraits all round the rooms for four generations back and coats of arms is over two doors of the Hall as in old English style. It seemed like perfect affectation...that everything should remain so old fashioned." It was probably not an eccentric urge to remain old fashioned that governed Hill Carter's taste so much as a respect for tradition. He represented the sixth generation of the Hill and Carter families to live at Shirley Plantation, and he undoubtedly looked with pride upon the old coats of arms and the four generations of portraits. Certainly it was not poverty that prevented him from bringing Shirley up to date. In her letter Julia Tyler noted, with some puzzlement, "And yet it cannot be on account of the expense that no change is made where it can be avoided, as we know how liberal the Carters are in other respects."

The liberality of the Carters and their adherence to the Virginia tradition of hospitality had been noted earlier by a young man fresh out of Yale, named Henry Barnard, who paid a visit to Shirley and observed the ebb and flow of guests and the Carters' skill as hosts. "When you awake in the morning," he wrote in a letter, "you are surprised to find that a servant has been in and without disturbing you, built up

The graceful ascent of a chimney in Shirley's kitchen echoes the design of the flying stairway in the house itself. Plantation kitchens were located in buildings separate from the mansions because of the fire hazard and also because the houses "by this means are kept more cool and sweet," in the words of one Virginian.

a large fire, taken out your clothes and brushed them, and done the same with your boots, brought in hot water to shave, and indeed stands ready to do your bidding." After an eight o'clock meal of Virginia ham, corn cakes, tea, and coffee, the guests were free to enjoy the diversions of the estate: "After breakfast visitors consult their pleasure—if they wish to ride, horses are ready at their command; read, there are books enough in the library; write, fire and writing materials are in his room."

The Carters tended to the business of the farm in the morning, but carriages full of guests might arrive as early as one in the afternoon for a three o'clock dinner of ham, beef, turkey, duck, eggs, and platters of vegetables. A round of toasts inevitably followed dinner: "After the glasses are all filled, the gentlemen pledge their services to the ladies, and down goes the wine; after the first and second glasses the ladies retire, and the gentlemen begin to circulate the bottle pretty briskly."

Before Hill Carter died, in 1875, he made certain that his oldest son, Robert, would take over the plantation so that it would remain in the family. Robert had other ideas at first. He had served in the Navy, become certified as sailing master, and looked forward to a life at sea. Robert's wife, Louise, remembered that Papa Hill Carter "tore and raved" until Robert gave up his plans and agreed to trod the traditional path of plantation master. In Louise's words, "It was ordained to be so."

The Carters' reverence for tradition has endured to the present. The tenth generation of the Hill and Carter line lives at Shirley today, farming the same acres that produced tobacco for the Hills in the seventeenth century. The generations of portraits look down upon the furniture and silver Charles Carter bought in the 1770s. Shirley remains the same "fine old place" Julia Tyler found so old fashioned because no Carter would ever try to conform to something as fleeting as modern fashion.

Shirley's river entrance is at the shore of the James, where the Carters built a wharf—now gone—for the ships that carried their tobacco to England. During the Civil War, after the battle at nearby Malvern Hill, wounded Union soldiers rested here until they were evacuated by boats.

The London silversmith John Carter made this neoclassical tea urn, with its reeded surface, elegant scroll handles, and matching salver, in 1774. Ordered for the wedding of John Parke Custis, Martha Washington's son by her first husband, it bears the Custis family coat of arms. Much of the Custis silver is now at Mount Vernon (Chapter Six); this urn and tray are kept in the west parlor.

This rococo five-bottle cruet stand was made by Jabez Daniel of London and purchased by George Washington in 1751. The caster with its pierced lid is part of an earlier set, made in 1736 by Samuel Wood.

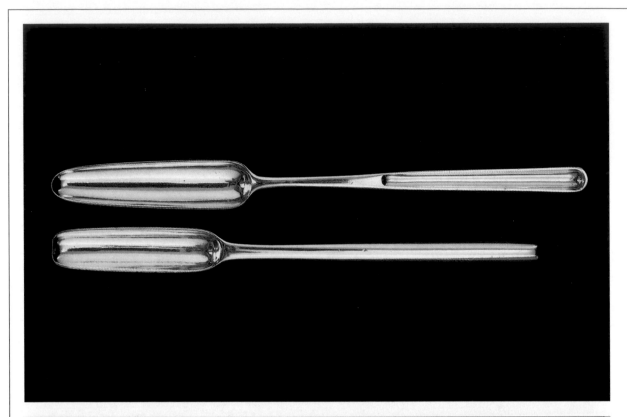

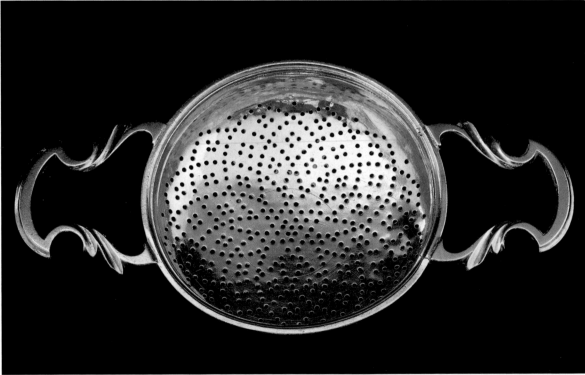

Slender spoons such as those at top were used to extract marrow from beef and venison bones. The smaller of them is made of a higher grade alloy called Brittania standard, which temporarily replaced sterling between 1697 and 1720. The strainer above, made in London in the late 1770s, removed seeds from fruit punches. All, along with the mustard pot opposite, belong to the Carters at Shirley Plantation (Chapter Two).

Lined in brilliant blue glass, its silver both pierced and engraved, this expertly crafted mustard pot was made about 1790 by the London silversmith William Plummer. The top is notched to accommodate a spoon.

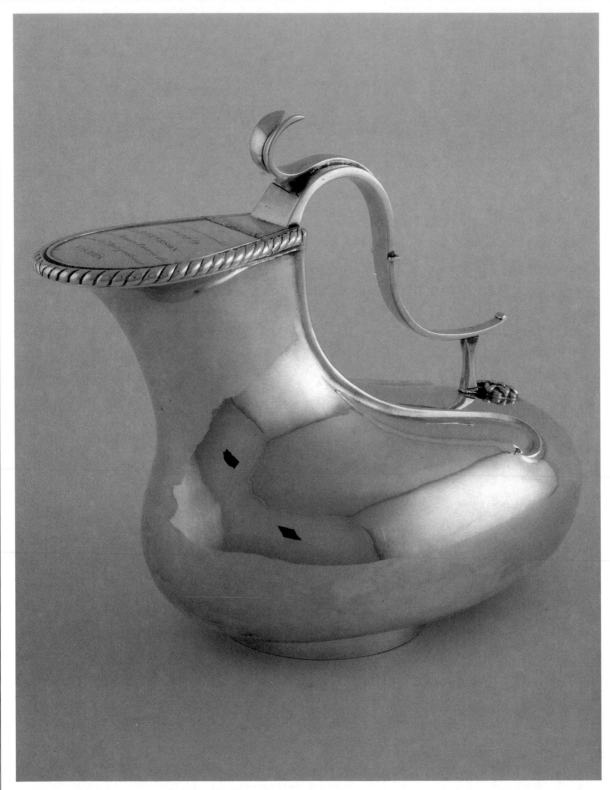

Thomas Jefferson designed this silver "askos"—a vessel for pouring wine—after seeing an ancient one made of bronze in France at the Roman temple at Nîmes. He commissioned a wooden model of the original and adapted its design to his needs by adding a lid and omitting some of the floral decoration. He had this version made to order from Simmons and Alexander of Philadelphia and used it at Monticello (Chapter Five).

This elegantly simple covered bowl was a gift from Thomas Jefferson to Camilla Franzoni, the wife of an Italian sculptor who was working on the capitol building in Washington. It was made by the Georgetown silversmith Charles Burnett about 1808 and engraved with the entwined letters **CF** *in a decorative cartouche. The bowl made its way back to the collection at Monticello through members of her family.*

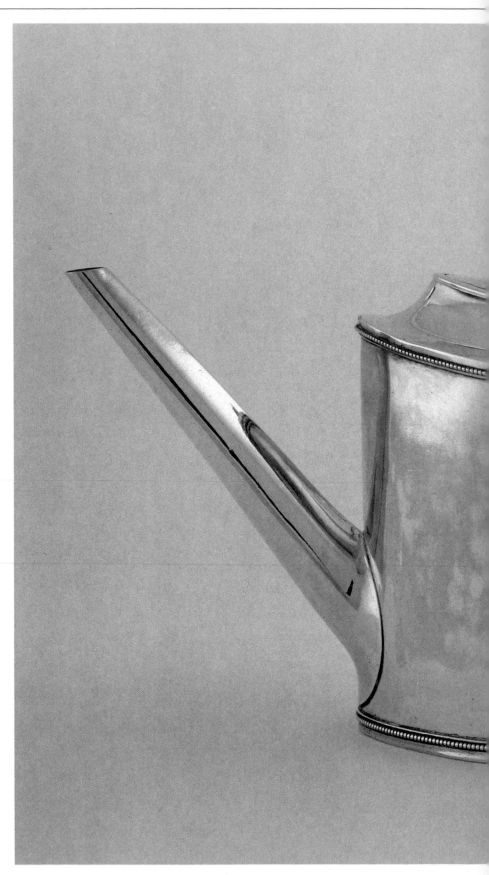

Made about 1790 by the New York silversmith William G. Forbes and engraved with the name Lee in a shield, this teapot is believed to have belonged to Light-Horse Harry Lee. Its simple and dignified design—elliptical shape, straight sides and spout—was popular on both sides of the Atlantic during the late eighteenth century.

The lion's mask and pendant handle were popular on large baroque silver pieces such as this monteith, a basin for chilling wine glasses. Made in London in the seventeenth century and now at Stratford Hall (Chapter One), this one has a detachable rim so that it can double as a punch bowl.

3

WILTON

THE ELEGANCE OF WOOD

Wilton is a house of subtle charms. From the restrained geometry of its facade to the refinement of its wood paneling, Wilton displays an elegance that is always muted, a wealth that does not call attention to itself, and a distinctly upper-class pride. It is solid and unpretentious, like the family that lived in it. Wilton was built in the early 1750s by William Randolph III and his wife, Anne Carter Harrison. It was one of a dozen Virginia mansions built by Randolphs—perhaps the most prosperous, influential, and prolific family in the colony. They were planters, ship owners, land developers and speculators, lawyers, and dedicated public servants.

Randolphs held public offices from justice of the peace to membership in the King's Council. There were three Randolph speakers of the House of Burgesses, and three attorneys general of the colony. Peyton Randolph was president of both Continental Congresses. Among their innumerable cousins and in-laws were some of Virginia's most eminent men, including Thomas Jefferson, whose mother was a Randolph. As a French traveler to Virginia in the early 1780s remarked, "You must be prepared to hear the name Randolph frequently mentioned." And an English traveler in the same decade found that the Randolphs "are so numerous that they are obliged, like the clans of Scotland to be distinguished by their places of residence." Among the Randolphs with the first name William were William Randolph of Chatsworth, William of Dungeness, William of Tuckahoe, William of Turkey Island, and William Randolph of Wilton.

Wilton was built about 1750 by William Randolph III. The facade of his house epitomizes the understated elegance so dear to the Virginians. Its only decorations are a classical doorway and edgings of rubbed bricks. During the Revolution Wilton was briefly the marquis de Lafayette's headquarters.

It was a Randolph tradition to marry within their class; they always had an eye on social connections and, of course, wealth. By these standards William III could not have found a better match than Anne Carter Harrison, daughter of Benjamin Harrison IV of Berkeley Plantation, near Shirley (Chapter Two) and Westover on the James River. Anne and William were married sometime between 1743 and 1745. The exact date is unknown because the marriage record has been lost.

Pierced scrolls decorate the stringer of the stairway in Wilton's entrance hall. The walnut balusters, three on each step, are turned and delicately spiraled. The stairway is the only woodwork in the house that was not painted.

It might be said that Wilton sprang from a bolt of lightning. In 1744 Benjamin Harrison and two of Anne's sisters were killed by lightning that hit a window at Berkeley just as Harrison was trying to close it. Shortly thereafter Anne's mother died, so Anne and William came into their inheritance sooner than expected. It was probably with the money from the Harrison estate that they purchased a tract of land called World's End on the north bank of the James, about ten miles below Richmond, where they built Wilton. Though some have said that the architect Richard Taliaferro had a hand in designing the house, the evidence is not conclusive, and it is possible that William Randolph was his own architect.

Wilton's exterior represents the less flamboyant vein of Georgian architecture, without any baroque flourishes or monumental Palladian elements such as porticoes and grand windows. Randolph opted for a simple doorway and a demure, low-pitched roof; but he enriched the simple brick facade with a subtle coloristic effect.

Opposite: In the entrance hall the carefully composed paneling by the stairs imparts a sense of graceful upward movement. The tall case clock in the hall is one of Simon Willard's finest pieces.

Overleaf: The parlor paneling, with its elaborately worked cornice and series of pilasters, is among the finest in Virginia. The furnishings include a rare pianoforte made in London in 1800 by John Broadwood & Sons. Only a dozen Broadwoods are known today. The piecrust tea table, made in New York between 1770 and 1785, is also rare. John Wollaston painted the portrait of William Randolph II, the father of the builder.

75

Along the corners and around the windows and doorway, he placed an edging of vermilion rubbed bricks, lending a cheerful lightness to a wall that might have been drab otherwise.

In contrast to the lack of embellishment on the facade of the house, Wilton's interior is striking. Randolph paneled the interiors throughout the house—every room, from floor to ceiling, including the closets. It was a very expensive undertaking, but not a particularly fashionable one. English and American designers had already begun to abandon paneling in favor of plaster walls, such as those at Kenmore (Chapter Four). Though Randolph was not the kind of man to be in the vanguard of style, he had a fine eye. The paneling he chose for Wilton was in the late baroque mode, in the style of the great British architect Sir Christopher Wren and Wren's master craftsman, Grinling Gibbons, in which raised surfaces and abundance of architectural detail impart a sense of movement to a flat surface.

The parlor of Wilton has been ranked among the most beautiful rooms in the country. Here the paneling displays its fullest visual effect, with fluted pilasters by the doorways and windows, arched alcoves flanking the fireplace, and a bold cornice atop the walls, all superbly carved. Randolph was careful about details. He ordered the marble fireplace carved in the same style as the paneling and made sure that his workmen concealed the pegs that hold the woodwork in place. An inscription found under a cornice in the parlor while the house was being renovated revealed that at least one of Randolph's craftsmen took pride in his work. "Samson Darrell put up this cornish in the year of our Lord 1753," says the workman's graffito, penciled into the wood in a successful bid for immortality.

The Randolphs had eight children, five sons and three daughters. Large families were the norm in Colonial Virginia, and Colonial mothers had to be adept at running large households. Though plantation houses such as Wilton had numerous slaves, many of these servants were, naturally enough, reluctant workers, who had to be coaxed and watched all the time. The mistress of the mansion had to be mistress of the vegetable garden, the icehouse, the root cellar, and the smokehouse.

Household management was the strong suit of the Randolph women. One of Anne's cousins, Molly Randolph, wrote a cookbook that set forth the principles by which Virginia ladies governed their domains. *The Virginia Housewife*, subtitled "The Methodical Cook," compared managing a house to running the ship of state: "The government of a family, bears a Lilliputian resemblance to the government of a nation." In addition to general guidelines such as "Let every thing be done at the

This mahogany desk-and-bookcase in the first floor office was fashioned by a New York cabinetmaker about 1775. An early-nineteenth-century inventory indicates that the piece belonged to the Randolphs.

proper time, keep every thing in its proper place, and put every thing to its proper use," Molly lays down some specific rules: "The contents of the Treasury must be known, and great care taken to keep the expenditures from being equal to the receipts." Everyone must sit down to breakfast together because "when the family breakfast by detachments, the table remains a tedious time; the servants are kept from their morning's meal, and a complete derangement takes place in the whole business of the day." While the servants are eating breakfast, the mistress should wash the glassware and begin preparations for dinner. "Order and regularity" bring "prosperity and happiness to the household"; and "methodical nicety . . . is the essence of true elegance."

William Randolph died in 1761, leaving substantial debts that may have resulted from the expense of building Wilton. Anne took over the house and the management of the estate. Of her life at Wilton little can be said with certainty. Just before and during the Revolution, she entertained distinguished visitors at Wilton. In the spring of 1775, George Washington stayed at the house after he attended the Virginia Convention in Richmond, where he heard Patrick Henry's defiant "Give me Liberty or give me death!" speech. For two weeks in May 1781, the marquis de Lafayette made Wilton his headquarters. The fields around the house were covered with the white tents of Lafayette's army, made up of units from New Jersey. Lafayette complained that he was unable to understand the New Jerseyans, not because his English was bad, but because *theirs* was.

Anne Randolph left no account of Lafayette's tumultuous stay at Wilton, when the house was crowded with officers; messengers were arriving in the middle of the

Overleaf: The office of a Virginia house often doubled as the gentlemen's smoking and game room. The English chess table, with ivory pieces, has a sliding board that can be reversed for backgammon, a more popular game than chess in Colonial Virginia. The sofa is in the style of Duncan Phyfe.

night; and the camp was in constant readiness lest Cornwallis and his British regulars make a sudden thrust from the south side of the James. Anne may also have had to endure the reproaches of her neighbors, many of whom resented the fact that Lafayette, a foreigner, was commanding American troops. Richmonders refused to lend him the horses his men desperately needed to keep a step ahead of Cornwallis. Anne's service to the Revolution at this critical point brought her the gratitude of George Washington, who entertained Anne at Mount Vernon (Chapter Six) after the war. In their parlor at Wilton, the Randolphs proudly displayed an engraving of the Washington family. In post-war Virginia it was a sign of status to be able to speak of the Washingtons as intimates.

Anne died in 1793. Her last years at Wilton were comfortable thanks to an income from her father's estate. The male Randolphs of Wilton did not adequately heed *The Virginia Housewife's* advice on monitoring the treasury. The debts of William Randolph III were not finally settled until 1797, and when William Randolph IV was master of Wilton in the early nineteenth century, he spent freely on silver, glassware, and furniture. The sumptuous furnishings seen today—purchased during the restoration of Wilton to replace the Randolph pieces that were dispersed in the nineteenth century—show Wilton as it was under William Randolph IV, who died in 1815. By the 1830s Wilton was in disrepair, and in 1859 the Randolphs sold the house to pay off debts. At the low point in its history, Wilton was a grain warehouse.

In the 1930s the owners of a factory adjacent to Wilton planned to remove the paneling to a museum and demolish the house in order to enlarge the plant. Virginians rallied to save the house William Randolph had so carefully built, and where Lafayette and Washington had unquestionably slept. Wilton was dismantled brick by brick, with a "methodical nicety" that a Randolph woman would have appreciated, and rebuilt on a new site in Richmond overlooking the James, where it stands today as the embodiment of Molly Randolph's ideal—"true elegance."

The master bedroom, on the first floor of the house, has Rhode Island furniture. The pierced-splat chair next to the bed was made by John Townsend, who may also have fashioned the bed itself. A very early Marseilles-type quilt with a phoenix design, made about 1790, covers the bed.

FURNISHING
THE NEW LAND

During most of the eighteenth century, Virginia families entertained in the parlor and arranged their most fashionable furniture in that room. Straight chairs and low-backed sofas were popular, being well suited to the formal conversation that was the chief entertainment of the day. In the typical parlor the fabric for upholstery and curtains matched, but Virginians were less rigid about the furniture itself—expensive mahogany chairs might be grouped with tea tables made of cheaper woods. In dining rooms a fine inlaid sideboard might have stood near tables made of ordinary pine.

Virginians bought their furniture from craftsmen in England and the northern colonies as well as from local cabinetmakers such as Peter Scott, who kept a shop in Williamsburg from 1722 to 1775. Furniture made in Virginia was strongly influenced by English styles, especially after pattern books published in London began to circulate here. The first of these, brought out in 1754 by Thomas Chippendale, contained ornate forms modeled after French rococo styles. Later in the century George Hepplewhite and Thomas Sheraton followed with books introducing simpler, neoclassical designs that, as interpreted by American makers, became known as the Federal style. But Colonial craftsmen were not merely imitators. The dog's-head carvings on Peter Scott's chair on page 86 and the wardrobe on page 89 do not appear in any pattern book and bear witness to the originality of Virginia cabinetmakers.

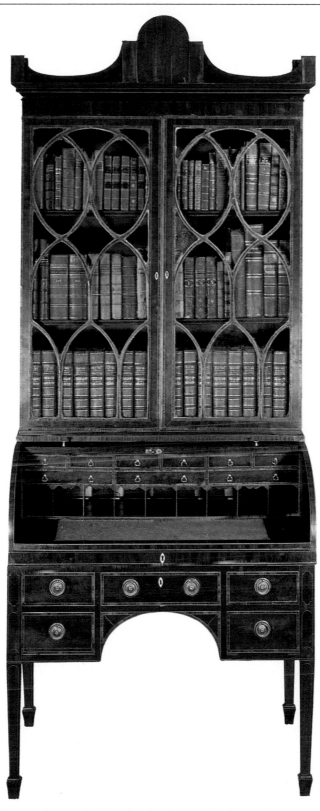

Crafted of mahogany, yellow poplar, and white pine in the Hepplewhite style, George Washington's secretary-bookcase was made about 1797 by John Aitken of Philadelphia. The fine tracery in its double doors and the arched kneehole are typical of the Federal period.

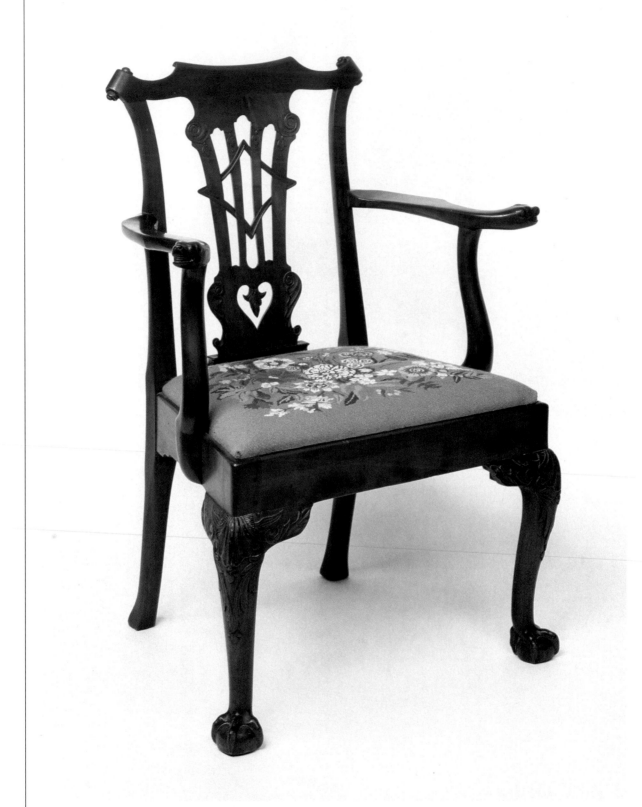

The dog's-head arms of this Chippendale chair identify it as the work of Peter Scott of Williamsburg. Made of cherry about 1745, it was among the original furnishings of Shirley Plantation (Chapter Two).

This Federal mahogany armchair from the dining room at Wilton (Chapter Three) is hand carved with an elegant fan design set in a heart-shaped back. It was one of a set made in Norfolk about 1790.

Made near Winchester, Virginia, in about 1810, the walnut-and-yellow-pine corner cupboard at left features an urn finial and, directly beneath it, a delicate teardrop inlay made of holly. The scroll pediment is decorated with another inlay, alternating light holly with dark mahogany in a pinwheel design that was popular with cabinetmakers in the Piedmont region. The cupboard, which is now at Wilton, probably stored a combination of ceramic, silver, and glass.

The wardrobe opposite, also from the Piedmont region, was made about 1760. The side compartment for books and other personal effects is highly unusual and was probably made to a customer's special order. The three drawers stored folded clothes; the upper part of the piece held clothes hung on hooks. The fittings are brass. The wardrobe, or clothespress as it was called, is now in the gentleman's bedroom at Kenmore (Chapter Four).

Nearly eight feet long, the Chippendale sofa at Stratford Hall (Chapter One) ranks among the most beautifully made sofas from the Colonial period. Virginia families, such as the Lees, who had relatives serving in Congress,

often ordered furniture from Northern makers: this one is the work of the Philadelphia artisan Jonathan Gostelowe.
The fabric here is a reproduction of a red Bingham damask popular at the time.

This clock by Simon Willard of Massachusetts is clearly his masterpiece: it stands nine and one-half feet tall instead of his usual eight, it is topped with urn-shaped brass finials instead of simple balls, and delicately carved Corinthian columns have replaced the plainer and more common Doric. Many of the clock's decorative touches allude to the passage of time. The jagged saw work along the top represents the sun's rays, and the inlay in the base of the clock shows a ladybug emerging from its shell. In the detail of the face, opposite, the four figures represent the seasons. On the face itself Willard added two extra dials—one for a second hand and another to record the day of the month. This extraordinary clock descended through the Robb family of Virginia and now stands in the entrance hall at Wilton.

4
KENMORE

A NEW MODE OF DECORATION

According to one of those family legends that seem to spring up around every Virginia mansion, before Betty Washington would consent to marry Fielding Lewis she made him promise to build her the finest house in the colony. Their home, now known by the name of Kenmore, more than fulfills that vow: in one respect—its richly decorated ceilings—it is without doubt the finest in America. In the dining room, in the parlor, and in the bedroom where Betty and Fielding slept, the ceilings are adorned with beautifully patterned plaster reliefs that some have compared to the decorative reliefs at Versailles.

When Betty and Fielding were married in 1751, she was only sixteen (one year younger than her brother George Washington); he was a twenty-four-year-old widower with an infant son, and a Fredericksburg merchant on the way up. The Rappahannock River carried oceangoing ships to Fredericks-

This portrait by John Wollaston depicts Fielding Lewis, a Fredericksburg merchant who built Kenmore in the 1750s, shortly after he married George Washington's sister, Betty.

burg, and Lewis took advantage of all the business opportunities a seaport offered to a shrewd and energetic young man. He shipped grain and tobacco for planters; dealt in fabrics, medicines, farming equipment, and a wide variety of luxuries imported from Europe; and sold provisions to ship captains. He planted his own

---

Kenmore has one of the simplest facades of all Virginia houses—it is the only Colonial brick house in the state without edgings of rubbed bricks. The lack of ornamentation suggests that Fielding Lewis originally intended to cover the facade with stucco but was unable to complete the project.

wheat and tobacco and speculated in land. Perhaps the most remarkable aspect of Fielding Lewis's business is that he considered Betty a full partner in all his enterprises, as the writer Susan L. Gauch recently discovered. They co-signed the papers in land transactions, and the barrels of tobacco they shipped to England bore the stamp FBL, for "Fielding and Betty Lewis."

When the Lewises were planning Kenmore in the 1750s, George Washington (then in his late teens) surveyed their

The overmantel in Kenmore's parlor depicts a scene from one of Aesop's fables—the story of the fox and the crow. According to family tradition George Washington suggested this fable for the overmantel. Its moral lesson is "beware of flatterers."

land for them and helped select a spot for the house at the top of a gentle slope that runs down to the Rappahannock about a mile away. Though close to the village of Fredericksburg, Kenmore was surrounded by the open fields of the Lewis plantation, bordered by a forest of oaks, hickories, and gums. In its ground plan Kenmore is similar to many other Colonial houses. There are four rooms and a hallway on both floors with a well-crafted staircase. Though the basic layout of Kenmore is not unusual, the decoration the Lewises chose for the interior was in the newest European style. They decided to plaster the walls rather than panel them as William Randolph had done at Wilton (Chapter Three), and to ornament the ceilings with plaster reliefs—a fashion that had lately come to England from Italy. It was a bold choice because until then plaster had been viewed as the poor man's wall finish, whereas paneling bespoke high style and wealth.

For reasons that are not known, the Lewises waited almost twenty years before they decorated the ceilings of the house. In 1775 they hired an itinerant French artist, whose name went unrecorded, to do the work. In the midst of the project, they

Opposite: Kenmore's plaster ceilings—the work of an unknown French artist—are the finest in any American house. On the parlor ceiling baskets of flowers and fruit, encircled by rosettes, surround the leaf medallion. Sinuous vines and beautifully sculpted cornucopias fill the panels outside the circle. As a whole the ceiling is a carefully planned geometric design of ovals and circles within circles.

Overleaf: In the master bedroom on the first floor, scallop shells and vines surround a basket of flowers and a festoon on the overmantel. The richly ornamented mantel is carved wood.

dispatched him to Mount Vernon, where he decorated two rooms for George Washington. Washington was away at the time so his manager, Lund Washington, supervised the work of the so-called stucco man, who exasperated Lund with his slow pace. Lund's progress reports to Washington are a little-known contribution to the literature of the warfare between overseer and workman. On September 29, 1775, Lund wrote, "The stoco man is still about the dining room and will I fear, be for some time." On October 5 he wrote, "Stucco workmen will be three weeks yet about the dining room," a prediction he had to revise on the fifteenth: "The stoco man thinks he shall be four weeks about the dining room.... It is altogether worked by hand which makes it tedious." On the twenty-second he wrote again, "The Stucco man is at work upon the dining room. God knows when he will get it done"; and on November 5: "The Man is still at it, and will be for a fortnight." A week later: "The dining room will I expect be finished this week.... The stucco man agrees the ceiling is a handsomer one than any of Colonel Lewis', although not half the work on it." Lund's impatience erupts in his note of November 24, "I have not yet got rid of the plasterer," but he was able to write with relief on December 10: "I have sent the plasterer back to Colonel Lewis. I think the dining room very pretty." As Lund realized, the work went so slowly because the stucco man had to mold every small element of the design by hand and press it meticulously into place.

The plasterer was being diplomatic when he told Lund that the Mount Vernon ceilings were better than his work for the Lewises. As fine as the Mount Vernon ceilings are, the Kenmore work is far superior in its elaborateness and size. Floral motifs—garlands, swags, bouquets sprouting from cornucopias, baskets of flowers, and delicate rosettes—appear in all three Kenmore ceilings arranged in striking circular patterns. In the dining room the face of a classical figure, perhaps a god, looks down from the center of a sunburst. Emblems of the four seasons appear in the corners of the bedroom ceiling: palms for spring, grapes for summer, acorns for autumn, and mistletoes for winter.

The stucco man also created plaster overmantels for the parlor and the bedroom. The bedroom's design—a basket of flowers and a garland—is in keeping with the style of the ceilings. The composition of the parlor panel, a scene from *Aesop's Fables*,

The motifs of crossed palm branches decorate a corner of the ceiling in the master bedroom. The palms, which symbolize spring, are one of four seasonal emblems on the ceiling. The French artist who made the ceilings may have taken these motifs from Batty Langley's City and Country Builder's Treasury.

differs from the rest of the work. Some regard this difference as evidence to support an old family story that George Washington suggested the theme for this mantel and

actually sketched an outline for it, which Fielding Lewis handed to the plasterer to follow. The fable that appears over the fireplace is one that would definitely have appealed to Washington the politician, familiar with the way powerful men can be manipulated. It is the fable of the fox and the crow, in which a crow has retreated to a tree to enjoy a piece of cheese. A fox wanders by and schemes to make off with the cheese, appealing to the crow's vanity by praising his lovely feathers and melodious singing voice. Since no one had ever compared his squawk to music before, the crow is charmed and decides to trill a song. As he opens his beak the cheese falls into the waiting jaws of the fox, illustrating the moral: beware of flatterers.

John Wollaston painted this portrait of Betty Lewis, the mistress of Kenmore, who bore a remarkable resemblance to her brother, George Washington.

The decoration of their ceilings was among the last extravagances Betty and Fielding could afford. During the Revolution they put all of their energy and money into supplying George Washington's armies. They built ships for the navy; provided gunpowder, lead, salt, flour, bacon, and clothing; and, most important of all, ran a gun factory. The Lewises financed the factory out of their own pocket and were never repaid. At the end of the war they were nearly broke, unable to pay the taxes on their house. Exhausted by his unremitting work during the war, Fielding died in 1781 just after the victory at Yorktown.

To Betty fell the tasks of managing the estate—a job that normally would have gone to a male relative, but Fielding had named her his executor together with their three sons—of caring for her sick mother, and of bringing up the children of her oldest son, who had spent all of his own and his wife's money. When the expense of maintaining Kenmore proved too great, she left the house, which was later sold by her son, and moved to a small farm where she could support herself and her family.

The canopied bed in the master bedroom originally belonged to the Lewis family. The white dimity hangings with white fringe make a pleasant contrast with the pompeian red color of the walls. Betty Lewis's household records show that she ordered a large amount of white dimity in the 1790s.

One upstairs bedroom at Kenmore has been furnished as a children's room, with a doll's cradle and toy soldiers. The soldiers are carved and painted pine, mounted on a flexible frame. Rag rugs, such as the one here, were often used in eighteenth-century houses. The Lewises had eleven children, only six of whom lived to maturity.

If she regretted the loss of her beautiful house, she was too proud to admit it. A letter she wrote to George reveals that she was stoic and independent: "I have not received a line from you since I left town, which place I was obliged to quit as I should most certainly have been ruined had I continued there one year more. This place…is poor, but…it will be of more advantage to me than the other."

Despite her difficulties she retained her sense of humor. To entertain the family she liked to make a joke of her remarkable resemblance to her famous brother. A relative remembered that she was "so strikingly like the brother that it was a matter of frolic to throw a cloak around her, and placing a military hat on her head, such was her amazing resemblance that on her appearance battalions would have presented arms and senates risen to do honor to the chief."

Her death was an ironic foreshadowing of her brother's. Both Betty and George worked until the very end of their lives, and both died from the rigors of outdoor labor. In the laconic account of a great-grandson, "While she was superintending some work on a mill one stormy day, Mrs. Lewis contracted a cold, and died on the thirty-first of March, 1797." No senates rose to do her honor at her death, and few history books mention the sacrifices Betty and her husband made on behalf of the Revolution. Their only memorial is their house, rescued from developers in the 1920s and painstakingly restored, a reminder of the graciousness and comfort that so many people of their time willingly gave up for the sake of independence.

Overleaf: The dining room is the only one that the Lewises decorated with paneling. The elaborate carving on the mantel includes the Washington crest—a swan and a crown. The room is furnished with a cherry-and-pine table, made in Williamsburg about 1745, and a Queen Anne looking glass.

According to tradition this tea set was presented to Alexander Hamilton by Count Rochambeau, commander of French troops fighting in the American Revolution. Made in France, the pieces are hand painted with views of farms, towns, or windmills—each is different. The set was passed down through several generations of the Hamilton family and now resides at Kenmore (Chapter Four) in Fredericksburg.

Jefferson bought this Sèvres porcelain monteith in France. He used it at Monticello (Chapter Five) to chill wine glasses and probably also to rinse them between courses as new wines were served.

This gilt-trimmed Worcester mantel vase is one of three sent to Mount Vernon (Chapter Six) by the Englishman Samuel Vaughan to ensure that his earlier gift—the mantel itself—would be properly set off. Each vase is painted with exotic scenes by Jefferyes O'Neale, an Irish miniaturist. The gentle faces of the lions in the detail opposite, from the painting on the reverse of this vase, are characteristic of O'Neale's work.

This punch bowl is the oldest and finest piece of Chinese porcelain known to have been owned by the Washingtons. Richly painted with pheasants, peacocks, chrysanthemums, and peonies, it dates from the mid-eighteenth century, before Chinese designs were influenced by the Western market. It is one of many punch bowls the Washingtons bought or received as gifts.

5

MONTICELLO

JEFFERSON'S MASTERPIECE

Monticello stands atop its mountain like the Platonic idea of a house; the perfect creation, existing in an ethereal realm, literally above the clouds. To reach it you must ascend "a steep, savage hill" through a thick forest of oaks and swirls of early morning mist that recede at the summit, as if by the command of the master of the mountain. The house that presents itself to view on the summit seems to contain some kind of wisdom in its very form. Even long familiarity as a national landmark and as the home of Thomas Jefferson has not dulled its impact. Seeing Monticello is like reading an old revolutionary manifesto—the emotions still rise.

In shape Monticello resembles nothing built in America in the eighteenth century. Jefferson disdained the boxy rectitude of the typical Georgian form and designed a dynamic house with indentations and protrusions—a geometric symphony of octagon, triangle, cylinder, and circle. It does not seem to have four walls and a roof; to walk around the house is to see an everchanging interplay of shapes. Over the western entrance to Monticello, he built a dome—the first one ever placed over an American house—in which a sphere merges with an octagon. It is difficult at first glance even to sense the exact location of a corner. From the outside there appears to be only one floor; in fact there are three. Jefferson placed the second-story windows at floor level and right above the first-floor windows, so they look to be one large window. The third floor, set back from the facades and invisible from below, is lit by skylights.

The fishpond in Thomas Jefferson's garden reflects the dome and western portico of Monticello, which was completed in 1809. "Mr. Jefferson is the first American who has consulted the fine arts to know how he should shelter himself from the weather," said one European visitor, the marquis de Chastellux.

In contrast to all this architectural novelty, the visitor would see at the entrance a classical portico—not just a few antique elements such as columns or a pediment inserted over the door, but a proper portico in the correct proportions. The juxtaposition might be saying that the classical world has provided a departure point, and a firm foundation, for flights of modern fancy.

Thomas Jefferson built Monticello when America was a new nation. Together with his designs for the state capitol at Richmond and the University of Virginia, his house was part of his attempt to devise a new form of architecture for the republic. In the architecture of ancient Rome, he found beauty and rationality (the two were closely linked in his mind), but he was too much an artist merely to copy antique forms. The entrance to his house is that of a temple, and around the tops of the rooms he displayed friezes based on Roman temple art; but his house has no echoing halls or dim sanctuaries. If the house is full of anything, it is full of a distinctly modern light: sunlight streaming through glass doors, skylights, and ample windows, reflecting from tall mirrors, illuminating everything, and banishing shadow.

Monticello was substantially finished in 1809 when Jefferson retired there from the presidency at age sixty-six. He was not the stooped scholar many people, even of his own time, have thought him to be. "He is quite tall," one visitor wrote with some surprise in 1814, "six feet, one or two inches, face streaked and speckled with red, light grey eyes, white hair.... His figure bony, long and with broad shoulders, a true Virginian." His overseer described him as "well proportioned, and straight as a gun barrel." He was an excellent horseman and liked to test his muscles on a dynamometer, a machine that measured strength. He could outpull men half his age.

His wife, Martha, had died in 1782 after ten years of marriage, but Monticello was never an empty house. His daughter Martha, her husband, Thomas Mann Randolph, and their eleven children lived with Jefferson at Monticello. He was a doting grandfather. One of his granddaughters recalled his climbing the cherry trees in the orchard and tossing down bunches to the children below. He organized footraces on the lawn, and in 1825, when financial problems were weighing heavily upon him, he ordered an expensive piano, from Currier and Gilbert of Boston, for

In the entrance hall Jefferson displayed the antlers of a moose and an elk given to him by Meriwether Lewis and William Clark, whom Jefferson had sent to explore the West when he was president. The fourteen-foot ladder in the corner, used when winding a wall clock, folds up into a single pole for storage.

a granddaughter in spite of Martha's protests.

In all it was a very happy retirement, if that word can be used to describe the active life Jefferson led until his eighties. He enjoyed farm work—he sang to himself as he rode around his fields—and was surrounded by his beloved family, his books, and the fruits of a lifetime of building and collecting.

The entrance hall of Monticello was Jefferson's museum. Here he displayed the objects of his wide-ranging fascination: artifacts the Lewis and Clark expedition had brought back from the West, mastodon bones unearthed in Kentucky, a model of the Great Pyramid of Egypt, American Indian paintings, a statue of a reclining Greek heroine, and curios such as a concave mirror that turns things upside down. The double glass doors at the end of the hall are among the Jeffersonian "gadgets" in the house that inspired one visitor to remark, "Everything has a whimsical and droll appearance." A chain below the floor connects the doors: when one of them is pushed open or shut, the other follows as if guided by an unseen hand. The mechanical doors open to a parlor that may have been the most elegant in the country in Jefferson's time. Jefferson installed one of the first parquet floors in America and hung his favorite paintings there. Nearly fifty pictures were displayed in this room in 1809. Some were portraits of family members and people he admired, others copies of works by Leonardo da Vinci, Raphael, Titian, and Rubens. Jefferson, however, did not consider himself a connoisseur of painting or sculpture and thought it slightly un-American to try to become one. America had too little money to spend it on pictures and statues. "It would be useless," he wrote, "and preposterous, for us to make ourselves connoisseurs in those arts."

The entrance hall and the parlor form the central axis of the house. To the north Jefferson placed the public rooms: dining room, tea room, and two guest bedrooms. Jefferson was often the first to arrive in the dining room for the three-thirty dinner. He kept a small reading table in the room so that he could make good use of his time while waiting for the family and guests to assemble. Since the pleasure of table talk was among his favorites, he disliked having servants popping in and out of the room during the meal. He also feared that the servants would hear snatches of conversation and repeat garbled versions of his opinions. One visitor who must have

Sunlight illuminates the parlor on the western side of Monticello, where Jefferson entertained guests. In the afternoon he played the violin here, accompanied on a harpsichord by his daughter Martha. On the right stands his "optique," a magnifying glass for viewing prints.

heard Jefferson discourse on this subject wrote that he believed "much of the domestic and even public discord was produced by the mutilated and misconstructed repetition of free conversation at dinner tables by these mute but not inattentive listeners."

Jefferson devised several ingenious ways to banish the servants from the dining room. He designed his own version of the English dumbwaiter, an aptly named set of shelves on rollers that held all the courses of the meal. At Monticello each diner had his own dumbwaiter and served himself. The servants placed hot food on shelves built into a revolving door in an alcove off the dining room. When the food was in place, the servant turned the door around without entering the room. The cleverest of all the dining room devices were two pulleys, concealed in the sides of the fireplace, that ran down to the wine cellar in the basement. When Jefferson needed to replenish the wine, he opened a narrow door in the fireplace, hauled up a bottle, and put the empty bottle in its place. All of these gadgets had the combined effect of making the dinner seem to appear by magic, at a wave of the master's wand.

Sliding glass doors separate the dining room from the tea room—a cozy retreat shaped like a half octagon, at the northern end of the house. Four windows virtually enclose the room in glass. Jefferson called this his "most honourable suite" because he displayed in this room busts of heroes of the Revolution—Washington, Franklin, John Paul Jones, Lafayette—and Roman emperors, implying that the great men of the eighteenth century deserved to stand in the pantheon alongside the great rulers of antiquity.

The southern wing of Monticello houses Jefferson's private quarters, a

"Music," Jefferson said, "is the favorite passion of my soul." He bought this mahogany piano for a granddaughter, and the maple-and-pine guitar for another granddaughter. He once considered forming a private orchestra by hiring farm workers who could also play instruments.

rambling L-shaped suite. It was a self-contained world, with his bedroom, study (which he called his cabinet), and library, all of which open onto each other through archways without doors. A piazza off the library contained a greenhouse and served as his private entrance to the suite. He referred to these rooms as his sanctum sanctorum and admitted almost no one to them.

He was a very early riser. It is said that he arose in summer as soon as there was enough light for him to make out the face of the clock. He dressed quickly, pulling his clothes from a revolving rack built into the wall of the bed alcove. Visitors noted that he was not fastidious about his clothes; he often wore a rumpled jacket made from the wool of his own sheep. In 1810 he described his daily routine: "My mornings," meaning the hours *before* breakfast, "are devoted to correspondence. From breakfast to dinner, I am in my shops, my garden, or on horseback among my farms; from dinner to dark, I give to society and recreation with my neighbors and friends; and from candle light to early bedtime, I read." Oddly enough, the man who surrounded himself with clocks recounted his schedule without a single reference to a specific time.

An avid collector of clocks, Jefferson probably purchased this Louis XVI marble-and-ormolu clock while he was in France in the 1780s. It stands on the parlor mantel, which is decorated with a frieze copied from a Roman temple.

He designed an alcove for his bed, enclosed at the head, foot, and above, but open on both sides. Depending on which side of the bed he got up on, he was either in his dressing room or in his cabinet. The alcove design took advantage of the principle that air moves more quickly through a narrow space. On the most stifling Virginia night, there was always a slight breeze blowing through his alcove to cool him.

Jefferson did most of his work in the cabinet, a sunny spot where he reclined in a chaise and wrote with a polygraph, a machine with two pens linked in such a way that the second pen made a copy of a document as Jefferson wrote with the first pen. His library of about six thousand books was undoubtedly the finest in private hands in America. One visitor from Boston went so far as to call it "without question the most valuable in the world." It included works on every subject of interest to Jefferson—classical and modern literature, architecture, history, economics, law,

---

Overleaf: The Jefferson family gathered in the dining room for their main meal at three-thirty. While waiting for dinner Jefferson read at the table on the left. He was one of the few men of his day who did not dismiss the women after dinner, when the conversation usually turned to serious topics.

diplomacy, and parliamentary procedure, for example. He had made a special effort to collect Americana when he had lived in Europe and kept standing orders in bookshops all over the Continent for French, Spanish, Portuguese, and Italian geographies and explorers' accounts.

In his time the library was not the neatly arranged room seen today. One of his slaves recollected that he worked amid piles of books, keeping twenty or more at hand by his chair. His collection overwhelmed the space allotted to it and engulfed other rooms. Jefferson's biographer Dumas Malone wrote that the eastern rooms of Monticello must have been "a forest of bookcases." He was a reader, not a bibliophile; he bought the cheapest editions so that he could afford to buy all the books he wanted.

Two narrow staircases tucked inconspicuously into passageways lead from the first floor to the second floor, where relatives and guests slept. The third floor holds Monticello's great mystery—the room under the dome on the western side of the house. Small circular windows admit light and give a panoramic view of the surrounding countryside. Known as the Sky Room, it is one of the most spectacular rooms in the house, but no one knows exactly what Jefferson planned to do with it. One relative wrote that he had planned to put a billiard table there, but a visitor who climbed the stairs to see it found the room given over to storage.

As an ensemble Monticello was brilliantly conceived. The house sits atop an underground complex of workrooms and storerooms linked by a long passage that runs underneath the house from one side of the hill to the other. Jefferson built dependencies into the hillside where they are open to the air and light but invisible from the house. He did not want his views cluttered by outbuildings after he had gone to so much trouble to build on a mountaintop. The site of Monticello is one of the revolutionary aspects of the house. No American had placed his home on a peak before Jefferson did; everyone else built by a river or a road where transportation was easy. His choice of a mountaintop site expressed the dual romantic and classicist nature in Jefferson. The Romans had put their country villas on hilltops, and Jefferson was an avid student of the Roman patrician way of life; but a love for the landscape, pure and simple, also inspired him to build where he did, despite the

One of the most pleasant rooms in Monticello, the tea room is a semioctagon with ornamentation inspired by Roman architecture. It looks out onto a pavilion and the gardens. A Parisian silversmith, Jacques-Louis-Auguste Leguay, made the coffeepot on the table by the window in the style of a classical vase.

mountaintop's shortage of water and the treacherous roads.

Jefferson regarded gardening among the fine arts; specifically he ranked it seventh after painting, sculpture, architecture, music, oratory, and rhetoric. He approached gardening with his characteristic blend of utter seriousness and utter joy. "There is not a sprig of grass," he said, "that shoots uninteresting to me." In his methodical fashion he sketched plans for flower beds and garden walks and made lists of the trees, shrubs, and flowers he intended to plant. One August afternoon he used his surveying instruments to plot the direct line of sight between Monticello and Carter's Mountain so that he could lay out his garden to be perpendicular to the line of sight.

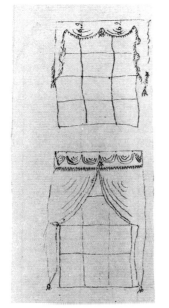

Jefferson gave his attention to every aspect of Monticello's decoration, including the shapes of the curtains. He sketched these designs as guides for a curtain maker.

The view from Monticello is best described in Jefferson's own words: "Where has Nature spread so rich a mantle under the eye? Mountains, rocks, rivers. With what majesty do we there ride above the storms! How sublime to look down into the workhouse of nature, to see her clouds, hail, snow, rain, thunder, all fabricated at our feet! and the glorious Sun, when rising as if out of a distant water, just gilding the top of the mountains and giving life to all nature!" Monticello is 530 feet high in the Blue Ridge Mountains, with a vast view of wooded ridges to the east and the long ridge of Carter's Mountain to the west. Jefferson owned Carter's Mountain, which he called Montalto, "the high mountain," because it was taller than Monticello, "the little mountain." Jefferson's romantic love of landscapes so possessed him that he cleared the trees from half of Montalto to make a pleasant meadow purely for viewing. He also drew up plans for a two-hundred-foot observation tower for the top of Montalto, but he never built it.

He transformed his own mountaintop into a garden in the sky, with a broad lawn on the west side of the house, surrounded by a serpentine walk dotted with oval beds of flowers. He built a brick-lined fish pool with a sitting stone, placing it so that a person sitting by the pool would see the reflection of the house in the water. On the

The book room was part of Jefferson's sanctum sanctorum, where he read, wrote, and drew up his architectural plans. The original furnishings in the room include the camera obscura on the table by the window, the architect's table by the other window, and the high-backed leather armchair.

hillsides below the house, he built four roads, in concentric loops with connecting paths, for horseback rides through the oak forest.

The creation of Monticello and its grounds took about sixteen years. Jefferson began building Monticello in 1796 by tearing down nearly all of the first house he had built on the site. It was modeled on Roman buildings Jefferson had seen only as illustrations in books, particularly Palladio's *Four Books of Architecture*. He decided to demolish his old house after a five-year stay in France, where he had seen the new style of less grandiose private architecture favored by the courtiers of Louis XVI. "All the new and good houses," Jefferson wrote, "are of a single story that is of the height of 16 or 18 [feet] generally, and the whole of it given to rooms of entertainment; but in the parts where they have bedrooms they have two tiers of them from 8 to 10 [feet] high each, with a small private staircase. By these means great staircases are avoided, which are expensive and occupy a space that would make a good room in every story." With this sentence Jefferson dismissed Virginians' propensity for building grand stairways.

The particular inspiration for Monticello was a house under construction while Jefferson was in Paris, the Hôtel de Salm. "While in Paris," he wrote, "I was violently smitten with the Hôtel de Salm and used to go to the Tuileries almost daily to look at it." It struck him as the perfect marriage of neoclassical style and intimate graciousness. In the Hôtel de Salm, and in the whole neoclassical ferment in France, Jefferson saw the outlines of an architecture appropriate to the New World. He had already turned to the classical world for a model. The architecture of ancient Greece and Rome was based on geometric notions of beauty—the parts of a building could be built to precise measurements in perfect proportion. The majestic march of a colonnade surmounted by the triangle of the pediment yielded a gracefulness that was not fortuitous, but the result of mathematical logic that could be understood and reproduced. As the Romans had emulated the Greeks, so Jefferson would study at the feet of the Romans, not as a dusty pedant, but as a passionate devotee. After seeing a Roman temple called the Maison Carrée, he wrote: "Here I am...gazing whole hours at the Maison Carrée, like a lover at his mistress."

He loathed the architecture of America because it was inherited from the

Jefferson's alcove bed stands between his bedroom, lit by a skylight, and his study. The doorway just visible on the right leads to a storage area for clothing above the bed, ventilated by the oval windows. In summer he arose as soon as there was enough light to see the clock on the shelf at the foot of the bed.

British. "Their architecture," he said, "is in the most wretched style I ever saw, not meaning to except America where it is bad, nor here in Virginia, where it is worse than any other part of America that I have seen." He referred to buildings in Williamsburg as "rude, misshapen piles" and grumbled that "the genius of architecture seems to have shed its maledictions over this land." His fervor may have blinded him to the genuine accomplishments of Virginia's builders, but it was an extremism in the defense of America's cultural liberty. In a letter to James Madison extolling the greatness of Roman architecture, he

Jefferson started a greenhouse in this glassed-in piazza on the south side of the house. He could enter the greenhouse from his book room, raise a window, and step onto the terrace in the foreground, which served as a promenade in good weather.

paused to explain himself: "You see that I am an enthusiast in the subject of the arts. But it is an enthusiasm of which I am not ashamed, as its object is to improve the taste of my countrymen, to increase their reputation, to reconcile to them the respect of the world, and procure them its praise." He planned to attain these ends by transplanting the flower of classical beauty to the independent climate of the New World. It took a man of Jefferson's genius to build a house that was an artistic and political manifesto and make it livable at the same time. In a house of geometrical and classical beauty, he provided comfort, convenience, fresh air, light, and space.

In 1824 Monticello was the setting for Jefferson's emotional reunion with an old comrade, the marquis de Lafayette, who was making a year-long triumphal tour of the United States. A mounted honor guard escorted the marquis' carriage up the winding road to Monticello past cheering crowds. The carriage stopped at the

Opposite: In the study Jefferson wrote in this chaise longue, fitted with candle holders on the arms, using a polygraph, which automatically copied a document as he wrote. He worked in this room from dawn until breakfast and again in the evening before going to bed. His telescope stands on the windowsill.

Overleaf: In the greenhouse Jefferson tried to grow trees and shrubs of the tropics—oranges, limes, acacias, and the fragrant and decorative mimosa. In the winter of 1810, the temperature in the greenhouse fell to twenty degrees, and his experiment in cultivating exotica came to a frosty end.

eastern portico of the house, where the two old revolutionaries met again after thirty-five years. Jefferson's grandson described the reunion: "The scene which followed was touching. Jefferson was feeble and tottering with age—Lafayette permanently lamed and broken in health.... As they approached each other, their uncertain gait quickened itself into a shuffling run, and exclaiming, 'Ah, Jefferson!' 'Ah, Lafayette!' they burst into tears as they fell into each other's arms. Among the four hundred men witnessing the scene there was not a dry eye—no sound save an occasional suppressed sob. The two old men entered the house as the crowd dispersed in profound silence."

At a banquet held at the University of Virginia in Lafayette's honor, Jefferson was too weak to stand and read his tribute. For several years he had been suffering painful attacks of rheumatism. In the summer of 1825, he was unable to leave the house much of the time, and in June of the following year, when Jefferson was eighty-three, he felt himself to be failing. His strength had ebbed and his digestion plagued him, but by a tremendous force of will he held off death until a day that he desperately wanted to see—July 4, 1826, the fiftieth anniversary of the Declaration of Independence. On its eve he awoke in the middle of the night and asked, "Is it the Fourth?" He died just after noon, at almost the exact time the declaration had been presented to the Continental Congress. He fulfilled a wish he had stated almost forty years earlier: "All my wishes end, where I hope my days will end, at Monticello."

On its peak at the fringe of the Blue Ridge Mountains, with its commanding view, Monticello inspired the marquis de Chastellux to write of Jefferson: "He had placed his mind, as he had done his house, on an elevated position, from which he might contemplate the universe."

DIVERSIONS OF
A RENAISSANCE MAN

Writing in *Travels in North America*, the marquis de Chastellux introduces Jefferson in a voice filled with wonder. "Let me then describe to you," he begins, "a man, not yet forty . . . an American, who, without ever having quit his country, is Musician, Draftsman, Surveyor, Astronomer, Natural Philosopher, Jurist, and Statesman." Jefferson's prominence as a statesman has tended to overshadow his other accomplishments, but the instruments on these pages offer ample evidence of his wide-ranging interests and abilities.

Jefferson often remarked that nature intended him to be a scientist, and his *Notes on the State of Virginia* begins as a scientific examination of his native state, based on records he kept of distances, altitudes, temperature, rainfall, plants, and animals. He loved any instrument that could assist him in his record keeping, and he visited the finest instrument makers in London and Philadelphia to obtain the most advanced models. Then, more often than not, Jefferson suggested improvements: he owned twelve polygraph machines, including the one on page 149, and each time he ordered one he specified changes he wanted made. More than the presidency, more than building Monticello (Chapter Five), Jefferson enjoyed his friendship with scientists and mathematicians and applying the principles of science to the practical concerns of a new and undeveloped nation.

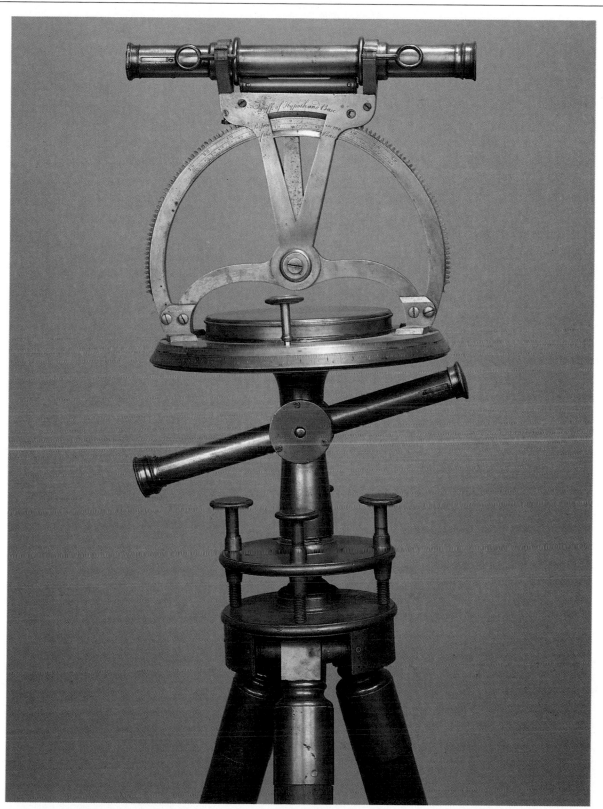

Mounted on its tripod is Jefferson's theodolite—the most sophisticated surveying instrument of its time. Made of brass and mahogany by the London instrument maker Jesse Ramsden, its movable upper telescope and fixed lower one measured both horizontal and vertical angles. Jefferson used this to survey his estate.

When hooked up to the wheel of a carriage, this instrument, called a "hodometer," measured distance in miles. It was made by the London instruments firm Nairne and Blunt, possibly to Jefferson's design— no others like it are known to exist. Jefferson used the hodometer to survey his lands and also to record distances between the cities that he visited.

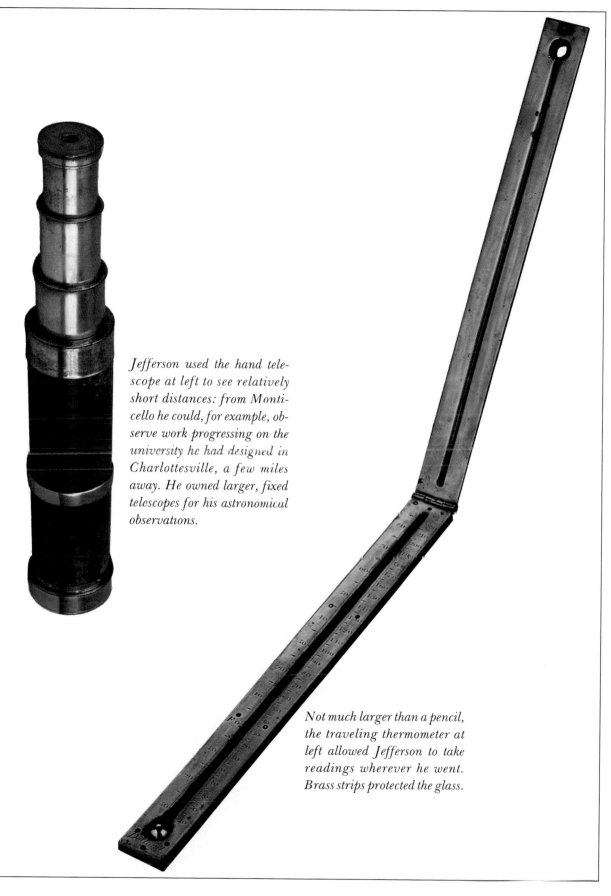

Jefferson used the hand telescope at left to see relatively
short distances: from Monticello he could, for example, ob-
serve work progressing on the
university he had designed in
Charlottesville, a few miles
away. He owned larger, fixed
telescopes for his astronomical
observations.

Not much larger than a pencil,
the traveling thermometer at
left allowed Jefferson to take
readings wherever he went.
Brass strips protected the glass.

Equipped with a strong magnifying glass, this instrument, called an "optique," was used to examine details of prints and engravings. Jefferson kept it in the parlor at Monticello for the enjoyment of family and guests.

This is Jefferson's camera obscura, which used a double convex lens to project a reduced image of an object on a screen inside the box. Made in 1800 by Philadelphia instrument maker David Rittenhouse, it was designed to help artists make accurate drawings of objects and silhouettes of people. Although Jefferson owned several of these machines, no drawings made from them have survived.

A tireless observer and record-
er of architecture, Jefferson
liked to sketch buildings he saw
on his travels around the
country. To make accurate
drawings he used a set of
drafting instruments like this
one, made of brass.

146

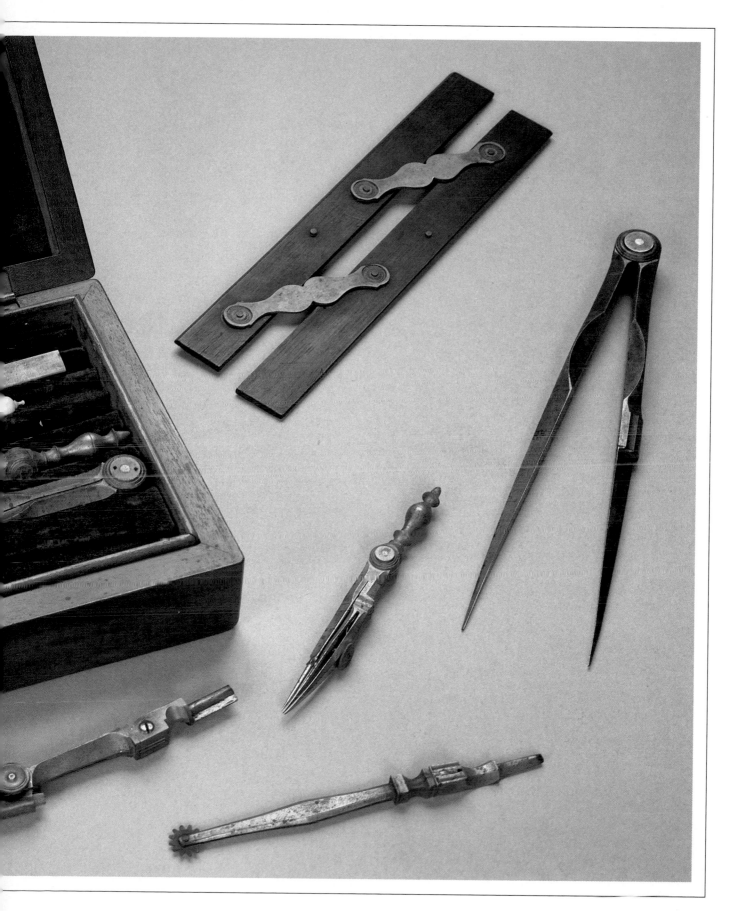

Jefferson devised this portable lap desk while he was serving as a delegate to the Continental Congress, so that he could work while on the road between Monticello and Philadelphia. Made of slender pieces of mahogany, the desk gave him a surface to write on as well as space to store paper, pens, ink, and sand for blotting. Jefferson ordered the desk from the Philadelphia cabinetmaker Benjamin Randolph in May of 1776. In the upstairs parlor of his rooming house, Jefferson used the lap desk to draft the Declaration of Independence.

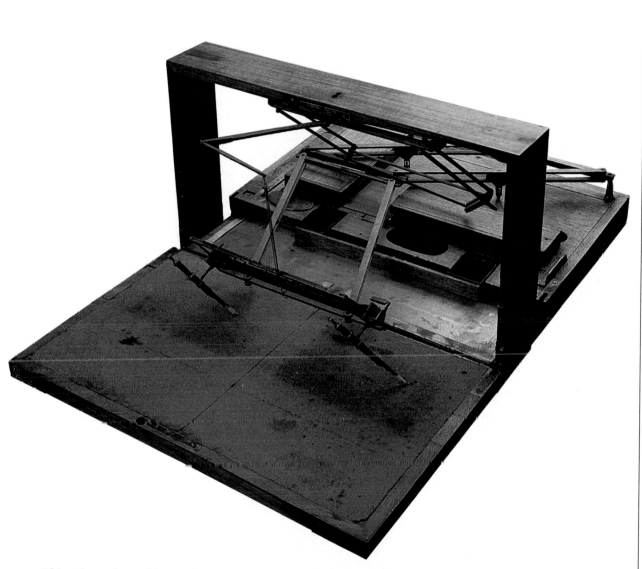

This polygraph machine made a copy of a document by the relatively simple expedient of attaching a second pen to the one held by the writer. Jefferson bought his first polygraph in 1804, the year it was invented, and owned at least twelve: he had realized the importance of preserving records as early as 1770, when a fire at his boyhood home destroyed all of his and his father's papers. Thanks to the polygraph, as well as to copying techniques available before it was invented, some sixty-six thousand of Jefferson's papers and letters survive.

6

MOUNT VERNON

WASHINGTON AT HOME

To the laurels he won as a general and a statesman, George Washington deserved to add another wreath, for architecture. Mount Vernon may not possess the complex beauty of Monticello or the imposing grace of Westover, but it nonetheless has the power to enchant. Like all great houses Mount Vernon is an ensemble: in Washington's grand design the landscape, gardens, walks, views, and house all work together to create a unified effect. Mount Vernon reveals a tranquillity, an affection for nature, an appreciation for the proper way to arrange things, and the palpable sense of a mind at work. "The good order of its master's mind appears extended to every thing around it," noticed one visitor in 1787, who exclaimed, "This is altogether the most charming seat I have seen in America."

Another guest, ten years later, was also amazed at what Washington had wrought so far from the centers of architectural taste in Europe. Count Julian Niemcewicz, a friend of the Revolutionary War hero Tadeusz Kosciuszko, noted in his diary, "The whole plantation, the garden, and the rest prove that a man born with natural taste may guess a beauty without ever having seen its model. The General has never left America; but when one sees his house and his home and his garden it seems as if he had copied the best examples of the grand old homesteads of England." The count

---

Opposite: With its dramatic view of the Potomac River, the piazza on the eastern side of Mount Vernon was one of George Washington's favorite places. He artfully landscaped the sloping grounds between the piazza and the river to frame the view with trees.

Overleaf: Washington added the broad, two-story-tall piazza to Mount Vernon during the Revolution, but his elegant design seems an integral part of the house. A Polish visitor, Count Julian Niemcewicz, noted that Washington liked to spend part of the afternoon here reading the newspapers.

was correct in seeing the reflection of English country palaces in Mount Vernon's broad white facade; but to use the word "copy" does an injustice to Washington's natural taste. The white exterior of the house—wooden boards cut and coated with sand to resemble courses of stone—does suggest the magnificent Palladian-style mansions of England, but Washington managed to drain the hauteur from the style while keeping the elegance.

Viewed from the entrance gate, across the bowling green Washington planted in front of the house, Mount Vernon has a pleasing rustic look. Curving colonnades, sheathed in red honeysuckle, branch out from the north and south sides and seem to disappear into the trees bordering the green. Washington planned this view with great care. The entrance road originally ran straight up to the door of the house. He removed it and substituted the bowling green, flanked by serpentine walks shaded by trees. Thus from the gate Mount Vernon appears framed in greenery; and from the house the eye roams over the bowling green to meadows and woods beyond. Another well-planned vista lies on the eastern side of the house. Mount Vernon stands on an eminence, 250 feet above the Potomac, with a commanding view of the broad river and the Maryland forests. In Washington's day white-sailed sloops filled

Benjamin Henry Latrobe visited Mount Vernon in 1796 and sketched the Washingtons on the piazza. Martha, her granddaughter Nelly, Washington's secretary (Tobias Lear), and Lear's son sit at tea while George watches the river traffic through a telescope.

the Potomac with their bustling commerce. During the Revolution Washington ordered a piazza built along the entire eastern length of the house to provide a comfortable vantage point. He removed trees and shrubs that blocked the view and planted locusts to frame the panorama. This was one of Washington's favorite spots. In the afternoon he would sit on the piazza with the newspapers (he received ten a day in the late 1790s), occasionally scanning the river with his telescope. The piazza was an architectural coup. Though many Virginia houses provided a fine view, no Virginia builder had thought to erect a proper place from which to see it. With no known precedent to guide him, Washington designed a broad and lofty colonnade in perfect harmony with the house and with the sweeping view it embraces.

Washington thought of himself as a plain-living man. Upon receiving a gift from an admirer, he remarked that it was "too elegant and costly by far I fear for

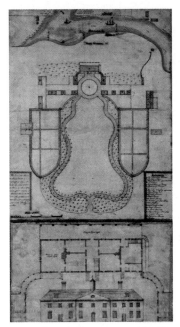

Samuel Vaughan prepared this map of Mount Vernon's grounds and a floor plan of the house itself during a visit in 1787.

my…republican style of living." While it is true that Mount Vernon's private apartments tend toward the Spartan, the formal rooms on the first floor display a refined taste and an appreciation for style. The small dining room, painted in the deep green shade that was Washington's favorite color—"grateful to the eye," as he saw it—is one of the rooms that display Washington's decorative instinct at its best. The carved chimneypiece is an exuberant rococo creation of leaves and scrolls that ascends to the ceiling, itself a masterpiece of the plasterer's art. The same unknown artist executed this ceiling and some of the magnificent ceilings at Kenmore (Chapter Four). In this room the artist was forced to work in an irregular space, and he triumphed over the odd angles of the ceiling with a design of delicate foliage surrounding a bold rosette.

Washington often whiled away an evening with friends at the card table in the west parlor across the hall. He had this room painted in another of his favorite colors, Prussian blue, which tends to mute the effect of the beautifully sculpted chimneypiece, similar to the one in the dining room. But here Washington added a broken pediment at the top of the piece, embracing the Washington coat of arms. A young George Washington looms over this room in a copy of the three-quarter-length portrait painted at Mount Vernon by Charles Willson Peale in 1772. Clad in the dashing blue-and-red uniform of a colonel in the Virginia Regiment, which he wore in the French and Indian War, Washington is every inch the young warrior who once remarked, "I heard the bullets whistle, and, believe me, there is something charming in the sound."

The west parlor is somewhat small compared to the usual Virginia parlor, but its size makes it the perfect vestibule for the large dining room, which is one of the finest rooms in America. It is two stories high and the length of the house, so that someone entering it from the west parlor immediately feels a sense of soaring space, a sense that is enhanced by the majestic Palladian window in the north wall. The three-part window serves as the centerpiece of a room that is an essay in architectural harmony and symmetry, as Washington's instructions to the builders reveal: "The chimney in the new room should be exactly in the middle of it—the doors and everything else to be exactly answerable and uniform—in short, I would have the

whole executed in a masterly manner."

The Adamesque decoration of the ceiling adds to the airy spaciousness of the room. The walls do not meet the ceiling at a right angle, but curve inward gracefully. These coves, as they are called, are adorned with delicate festoons. Equally delicate farming motifs—a scythe, a sheaf of wheat, a pick, and a shovel—decorate the ceiling itself. In the center exquisite foliage surrounds a sunburst.

To Washington's careful planning serendipity put the last graceful touch—the elegant marble chimneypiece known as the Vaughan mantel. Samuel Vaughan was a successful British merchant who married an American, settled in the United States after the Revolution, and cherished an abiding admiration for the father of American liberty. Vaughan met Washington in 1783 and must have proved a congenial acquaintance because Washington filled his ear with descriptions of Mount Vernon. They discussed wallpaper designs for the new dining room, and Washington must have told Vaughan that the room still lacked an appropriate chimneypiece. Vaughan made Washington a gift of the superb mantel that was the pride of his house back in England. He wrote to his son to remove the mantel, crate it up, and dispatch it to Virginia. This is the gift that provoked Washington's well-known protestation of modesty: "I have the honour to inform you that the chimney-piece is arrived, and by the number of cases (ten) too elegant and costly by far I fear for my room and republican style of living."

The most private room on the first floor was Washington's study. At dawn in summer, and well before sunrise in winter, Washington descended the private stairway from the bedroom to this room, washed at a dressing table by the wall, and set to work on his household accounts and correspondence. The room Washington considered to be most his own, where he spent many solitary hours, displays not a single decorative flourish. A portrait of his beloved half brother, Lawrence, hung on one wall. On a shelf over a doorway in a corner—perhaps the most inconspicuous place in the house—Washington placed the bust Houdon made of him, now

Opposite: In its very simplicity the passage is one of the finest in Virginia. The pine paneling is "grained"—painted to simulate mahogany—a decorative technique common in the eighteenth century.

Overleaf: Washington renovated the west parlor in the 1750s, transforming it into a formal room with pilasters and a pediment around the doorway and a rococo chimneypiece, which is based on a design he had seen in a builder's guidebook. Washington ordered the painting over the mantel from England. He specified the size but left the subject vague, saying only that he wanted a "neat landscape."

exhibited in the museum at Mount Vernon.

The second floor of Mount Vernon holds six bedrooms, all simply furnished. The master bedroom, above the study, contains the bed where Washington died, Martha's desk and dressing table, a few small tables, and family portraits.

One of the remarkable things about Mount Vernon is its unity. Washington did not have the luxury of building Mount Vernon all at once: it grew in stages. Yet the house betrays few signs of its piecemeal construction and decoration, despite the fact that Washington began the renovation when he was a young man of twenty-five, whose main education had been in woodsman's lore and Indian fighting, and completed it in his sixties, when he had seen the elegant houses of Philadelphia, New York, and Boston. As Niemcewicz noted, he was born with natural taste and never wavered from it.

The dining room's Palladian window is equally striking from the outside, with a broken pediment and pairs of pilasters. The entire facade appears to be stone, but it is actually made of boards shaped to resemble stones and coated with sand for durability.

In the 1730s Washington's father, Augustine, built the original eleven-room, one-and-a-half story cottage, which was inherited by Lawrence Washington. George rented Mount Vernon and its 2,300 acres of tobacco fields from Lawrence's widow in 1754. He came into the title and full possession upon her death in 1761. In 1757, when he was serving in the militia, guarding Virginia's frontier from Indian attacks, he was already dreaming of parlors, parties, and evenings by the fireplace with a gentle wife. "I have been posted for twenty months past upon our cold and barren frontiers," he wrote in the spring of 1757 to a buyer in London, requesting supplies for Mount Vernon, including a landscape for the mantel in the west parlor. During a visit home he had sat down with Abraham Swan's *British Architect,* a new builder's guidebook published in 1745, and selected the design for the west parlor chimneypiece, which he toned

A three-part Palladian window dominates the large dining room, with a lofty central window arching into the cove above it. The Sheraton chairs are pushed back against the wall as they would have been in Washington's time whenever they were not being used.

down a bit, creating the chimneypiece that stands in the parlor today. Anticipating marriage and a family, he raised the roof of Mount Vernon to create a second floor of bedrooms. The work was still going on when he brought home his bride, the widow Martha Custis, and her two children, Patsy and Jacky. "I am now I believe," he wrote, "fixed at this seat with an agreeable consort for life and hope to find more happiness in retirement than I ever experienced amidst a wide and bustling world."

The beautiful marble mantel in the large dining room was given to Washington by an English admirer, Samuel Vaughan, who also presented him with the three Worcester porcelain vases that stand on the mantel.

He was twenty-seven.

Washington made his next major renovations in 1773, when he decided to add the study at the southern end of the house and the large dining room on the north—additions that would more than double the size of Mount Vernon. The house was abuzz with workmen in 1775 when a "clash of resounding arms," in Patrick Henry's phrase, was heard from the north. In May 1775 he rode to Philadelphia for the meeting of the Continental Congress, reluctantly leaving the renovation still in progress, but anticipating that he would be back in July. It was six years before he saw Mount Vernon again. The Congress elected him commander in chief, and he rode off immediately to Boston. He informed Martha of the decision in a letter, in which he enclosed his will. To his brother he wrote, "I am now to bid adieu to you, and to every kind of domestic ease for a while." He left Martha and the plantation in the care of his cousin Lund Washington, who managed Mount Vernon throughout the war.

Lund and Washington wrote to each other constantly during the war. Lund's

Opposite: In one of three carved panels in the Vaughan mantel, a young girl draws water from a well. The panels are fashioned from marble, and the gracefully fluted column is of brown jasper. The mantel's farming scenes complement the agricultural motifs Washington chose for the ceiling of the room.

Overleaf: The mahogany table in the small dining room was once owned by Martha's granddaughter Nelly and may be an original Mount Vernon piece. The blue-and-white Canton china is part of a set that Martha presented to a close friend, Mrs. Samuel Powel, in Philadelphia.

letters were a litany of disasters, mishaps, reports of bad weather, and excuses. Workmen lazed about or drank, or did not show up at all: "There is a rascal in Alexandria that has promised to come every week for three months past." A carpenter nearly chopped his own foot off. The weather brought farm work to a halt: "Never was there more rain of a summer than this." Through it all Washington wrote letters from his various headquarters giving Lund the minutest instructions. In 1781 he wrote, "How many lambs have you got this spring? How many colts are you like to have?... Have you any prospect of getting paint and oil? Are you going to repair the pavement of the piazza?" Clearly the general was homesick.

Except for a brief visit in 1781, Washington did not see Mount Vernon until 1783. He returned, at a hard gallop, on Christmas Eve, his happiness complete. "At length, my dear marquis," he wrote to Lafayette, "I am become a private citizen on the banks of the Potomac and under the shadow of my own vine and my own fig tree; free from the bustle of a camp and the busy scenes of public life." He did not expect that the busy scenes of public life would descend upon him at Mount Vernon. Washington was America's first celebrity, and Mount Vernon one of the first places to which Americans felt they had to make a secular pilgrimage. The house was inundated with guests—neighbors, relatives, a variety of visitors bearing letters of introduction from mutual acquaintances, and a parade of curiosity seekers who simply showed up and expected to be fed. In exasperation Washington referred to his house as "a well-resorted tavern." One night he noted in his diary that he and Martha had sat down to dinner by themselves for the first time in twenty years. But not all guests were unwanted. A young Noah Webster dropped in; Lafayette visited twice; and Light-Horse Harry Lee came frequently.

In the spring of 1789, at the time of year when Mount Vernon was most delightful, its gardens bursting with colors and scents, duty called Washington away once again. He had been elected the first president of the United States, but the honor did not compensate for the pain of exile from his home. He felt like "a culprit who is going to

---

Opposite: This bedroom on the third floor accommodated overnight visitors when the five second-floor guest rooms were full. The room is very simply furnished with Windsor chairs and a footstool.

Overleaf: For several hours each day, and all day Sunday, Washington retired to this room to work on his correspondence. His letterpress, which made a copy of a document by pressing a moistened blank page against the original, stands on a table at the left. In the corner is a fan chair: a foot pedal caused the fan over the seat to move back and forth, sending a slight breeze over the sitter.

the place of his execution; so unwilling am I, in the evening of a life nearly consumed in public cares, to quit a peaceful abode for an ocean of difficulties." His two terms in office, in the early capitals, New York and Philadelphia, kept him away from Mount Vernon for eight years.

Count Niemcewicz visited him in June 1798, when Washington had retired to his plantation for good. Washington led his guest through his gardens, fragrant with the scent of magnolia, "the pleasantest smell I have ever noticed," wrote Niemcewicz. In the evening the whole family sat on the piazza to watch the sunset cast a lavender afterglow over the Potomac.

Niemcewicz found that Washington, at the age of sixty-six, had not altered the rigorous routine of his farming life. He rose early, worked at his desk until breakfast at seven-thirty, then rode off on the twenty-mile circuit of his farms. He returned for dinner at three o'clock and spent the evening with his family and the inevitable guests. He retired at nine. Foul weather never kept him inside. One morning in December 1799, he rode out into a snowstorm to cut down some trees that blocked his views. That night he awakened with a sore throat so severe he could barely breathe. His doctors were summoned and bled him, at his own insistence, but their treatments were no help. On December 14 he died in his bed, probably of a severe infection. At his request he was buried at Mount Vernon, though Congress did try to have him buried in the new capital, already named Washington.

Harry Lee's famous eulogy for Washington contains a revealing line that is not often remembered. Lee was an intimate of Washington's, and well knew that there was more to him than had met the public eye. After the famed paean "First in war, first in peace, and first in the hearts of his countrymen," Lee went on, "he was second to none in the humble and endearing scenes of private life."

Washington carried the trunk at the foot of the bed with him on his campaigns during the Revolution. He died in this bed on the night of December 14, 1799. Martha Washington sat by stoically while Tobias Lear stood next to him and held his hand.

Acknowledgments

The Editors would like to thank the following for their assistance: Mrs. Walker Allard, custodian of historic buildings, Stratford Hall; William Beiswanger, architectural historian, Monticello; Scott F. Burrell, assistant manager, Virginia House; Mr. and Mrs. C. Hill Carter, Shirley; Jane Colihan; W. Vernon Edenfield, director, Kenmore; Mr. and Mrs. Frederick Fisher, Westover; Matthew V. Gaffney, director of public programs, Monticello; Charles Granquist, assistant director, Monticello; Mrs. Judy Hynson, custodian of records, Stratford Hall; Malcolm Jamieson, Berkeley; Calder C. Loth, senior architectural historian, Virginia Historic Landmarks Commission; Kathy Malone, assistant professor, Department of History, Pacific Lutheran University, Tacoma, Washington; Christine Meadows, curator, Mount Vernon; Mount Vernon Ladies' Association; Elizabeth Panhorst, curator, Kenmore; Colonel James C. Sutherland, assistant executive director, Stratford Hall; Thomas Jefferson Memorial Foundation, Monticello.

Credits

Page 8: Metropolitan Museum of Art, Gift of Edgar William and Bernice Chrysler Garbisch, 1963. 10: Katherine Wetzel, courtesy Wilton. 11: The Mariners' Museum. 12: Colonial Williamsburg Photograph. 13: David Sweet. 14: Maryland Historical Society, Baltimore. 15: National Gallery of Art, Washington, D.C.; Gift of Edgar William and Bernice Chrysler Garbisch, 1953. 20, 32: Stratford Hall. 37: Courtesy Mount Vernon Ladies' Association. 38–43: Derek Fell. 46: Taylor Lewis. 61–63: Paul Rocheleau/Mount Vernon Ladies' Association. 64–65: Paul Rocheleau/Shirley. 66–67: Paul Rocheleau/Monticello. 68–71: Paul Rocheleau/Stratford Hall. 85: Courtesy Mount Vernon Ladies' Association. 86: Paul Rocheleau/Shirley. 87–88: Paul Rocheleau/Wilton. 89: Paul Rocheleau/Kenmore. 90–91: Paul Rocheleau/Stratford Hall. 92–93: Paul Rocheleau/Wilton. 109: Paul Rocheleau/Shirley. 110–111: Paul Rocheleau/Kenmore. 112–113: Paul Rocheleau/Monticello. 114–117: Courtesy Mount Vernon Ladies' Association. 131: Massachusetts Historical Society. 141–142, 143 (left): Paul Rocheleau/Monticello. 143 (right): Smithsonian Institution. 144–147: Paul Rocheleau/Monticello. 148: Smithsonian Institution. 149: Paul Rocheleau/Monticello. 154–155: Courtesy Mount Vernon Ladies' Association.

All other photos, including the cover, are by Paul Rocheleau.

Index
Page numbers set in *italic* refer to captions.

Adam, James, 10
Adam, Robert, 10
Adams, John, 17
Agecroft Hall, garden at, *36, 40*
agriculture
    of gardens, *36*
    of plantations, 12–13
    of tobacco, 11
Aitken, John, *85*
American Revolution, 15
    Lee family in, 17–20, 29–31
    Fielding and Betty Lewis during, 10
    G. Washington in, 163–167
    Wilton during, *73,* 79–80
Anthony, Joseph, *61*
architects, 10
architecture
    English books on, 10–11
    Georgian, 9–10
    Jefferson on, 132–135
    of Kenmore, *94,* 97
    of Monticello, 118–121
    of Mount Vernon, 154–157
    Palladian windows, *161*
    of plantation houses, 7
    of plantations, *8*
    of Shirley Plantation, 46, *46,* 49, 56
    of Stratford Hall, 17–21
    of Wilton, 73–78, *73*
    Wren's, 8–9
art
    collected by Jefferson, 123
    of dining, *108–117*
    of furniture, *84–93*
    of Kenmore ceilings, *97,* 101–102
    of silversmithing, *60–71*

Barnard, Henry, 56–58
baroque architecture, 8–10, 78

baroque style of silversmithing, *60*
Beverley, Robert, 7, 9
Boorstin, Daniel, 15
brick, 8–9
Britain, *see* England
Brittania standard (silver), *64*
Broadwood, John, *75*
Burnaby, Andrew, 7, 14
Burnett, Charles, *67*
Byrd, William, II, 13–15, *13,* 49
Byrd, William, III, 49–52

camera obscura, *145*
Campbell, Colin, 11
Caroline (queen, England), *25*
Carter, Ann Hill, *17,* 31
Carter, Charles, *49,* 52–53
Carter, Elizabeth, 49–52
Carter, Elizabeth Hill, 46–52, *46, 53*
Carter, Hill, *46,* 53–58
Carter, John, 46–52, *46, 60,* 62
Carter, Landon, 52
Carter, Louise, 58
Carter, Robert, 58
Carter, Robert "King," 13, *46,* 49, *49*
Carter family, 14–15, 56, 58
    Shirley Plantation of, *9*
    silver owned by, *64*
    Wedgwood stoneware of, *109*
Carter's Mountain (Virginia), 131
Case, John, *25*
ceilings, at Kenmore, 94–102, *97*
Chastellux, Marquis François Jean de, *118, 138, 140*
Chinese porcelain, *108, 117, 163*

Chippendale, Thomas, *84*
Chippendale furniture, *21, 25, 85, 90–91*
    in Stratford Hall, *33*
Civil War
    Robert E. Lee in, 32
    Shirley Plantation in, *58*
Clark, William, *121,* 123
clocks, *75, 92, 125*
Cocke, Bowler, 52
Colonial architecture, *94*
Colonial Virginia, 7–15
Continental Congresses, 73, *148,* 163
Cornwallis, Charles, 82
Custis, Jacky, 163
Custis, John Parker, *62*
Custis, Patsy, 163

dancing, 15
Daniel, Jabez, *63*
Darrell, Samson, 78
dishes, *108–117*
drafting instruments, *146*

England
    architecture of, 8–10, 132–135
    furniture imported from, *84*
    porcelain from, *108*
    Revolution against, 15–20
    Virginia settled by, 11

Fairfax family, 20
families, 78
Federal style of furniture, *84, 87*
Fithian, Philip Vickers, 14–15, 25–29
Fitzhugh, William, *60*
floors, at Monticello, 123
Forbes, William G., *68*
fox hunting, *15,* 25

Franzoni, Camilla, *67*
funeral hatchments, *49*
furniture, *84–93*
  Jefferson's, *135*
  at Kenmore, *102–107*
  at Mount Vernon, *161, 163, 167*
  at Shirley Plantation, 49, *53*
  at Stratford Hall, *21, 25, 29, 31, 33*
  at Wilton, *75, 79, 82*

gambling, 14, *14*
games, *79*
gardens, *36–45*
  at Monticello, *118*, 131
Gauch, Susan L., 97
Geddy, James, *60*
Georgian architecture, *9–10*
Gibbs, James, 11
Gloucester (Virginia), *11*
Gostelowe, Jonathan, *90–91*
government of Colonial Virginia, 12
Governor's Palace (Williamsburg), 8, *12*
Great Britain, *see* England
Great Hall (Stratford Hall), 21, *21*, 25
Greek architecture, 132
Gunston Hall, garden at, *38–39*

Hamilton, Alexander,   *110*
Harrison, Anne Carter, 73, 75, 79–82
Harrison, Benjamin, IV, 75
Henry, Patrick, 32, 79, 163
Hepplewhite, George, *84*
  furniture style of, *25, 85*
Hill family, 46, 58
hodometer, *142*
horse races, 25
Hôtel de Salm (Paris), 132
Houdon, Jean Antoine, 157–161

House of Burgesses (Virginia), 12, 73
houses
  gardens attached to, *36*
  Kenmore, 94–105
  Monticello, 118–138
  Mount Vernon, 7, 151–171
  Shirley Plantation, *9*, 46–58
  Stratford Hall, 17–32
  Wilton, 73–82
hunting, *15*, 25

Indians, 11, 21
interior decoration
  of Kenmore, 97
  late eighteenth century, 9

James River, 11, *11*
Jamestown (Virginia), 11
Jefferson, Martha (daughter; Randolph), 121–123, *123*
Jefferson, Martha (mother), 121
Jefferson, Thomas, 8, 73, 121–131, *131*
  alcove bed of, *132*
  on architecture, 132–135
  Chastellux on, *138*
  garden of, *36, 44–45*
  greenhouse of, *135*
  Monticello built by, 118–121, *118*, 132–135
  porcelain of, *113*
  scientific instruments of, *141–149*
  as scientist, *140*
  silver owned by, *66, 67*
Jones, Inigo, 10

Kenmore, 10, 94–105
  bedrooms in, *102–104*
  ceilings at, *97*
  dining room of, *105*
  facade of, *94*
  furniture at, *88*

  stoneware at, *110*
King's Council (Virginia), 12, 21–25, 29, 49, 73
kitchens
  for Shirley Plantation, *56*
  for Stratford Hall, *33*
Kneller, Godfrey, *46*
Kosciuszko, Tadeusz, 151

Lafayette, Marquis Marie de, *73*, 79–82, 135–138, 167
landscaping, 20
Langley, Batty, 11, *101*
lap desk, *148*
Latrobe, Benjamin Henry, *14*, 37, *154*
Lear, Tobias, *154, 171*
Lee, Ann Carter, *29*, 53
Lee, Arthur, 17
Lee, Flora, 29
Lee, Francis, 17, 20
Lee, Hannah Ludwell, 21, *29*
Lee, Light-Horse Harry, *17*, 31–32, *32*, 53, 68, 167, 171
Lee, Matilda, 29–31, *32*
Lee, Philip Ludwell, 25, 29
Lee, Richard Henry, 17–20, 25–31
Lee, Robert E., *17*, 25, 29, 31, 32, 53
Lee, Thomas, 17, *17*, 20, 21–25, *25*
  Stratford Hall built by, 9, 20
Lee, William, 17
Lee family, 15–32, *29*
Leguay, Jacques-Louis-Auguste, *129*
letterpress, Washington's, *167*
Lewis, Betty Washington, 94, 97, 102–105, *102*
Lewis, Fielding, 94–101, *94*
Lewis, Meriwether, *121*, 123
libraries, Jefferson's, 125–129

Louis XVI (king, France), 132

Madison, James, 135
Maison Carrée (Nîmes, France), 132
Malone, Dumas, 129
Mason, George, *36, 38–39*
Monticello, 118–138, *123, 131,* 138
  bedroom in, *132*
  dining room at, *125*
  entrance hall for, *121*
  fishpond at, *118*
  garden at, *36, 44–45*
  greenhouse at, *135*
  porcelain at, *113*
  silver at, *66, 67*
  tea room of, *129*
Mount Airy, 10
Mount Vernon, 7, 10, 151–171, *151*
  bedrooms in, *167, 171*
  ceilings at, 101
  garden at, *36, 37*
  Anne Carter Harrison at, 82
  map of, *155*
  Palladian windows of, *161*
  paneling of, *157*
  piazza of, *151, 154*
  silver at, *62*
  stoneware at, *113*
  Vaughan mantel in, *163*
  west parlor of, *157*
music, Jefferson on, *124*

Navigation Acts (Britain, 1660s), 11
Nestor (horse), *49, 53*
Niemcewicz, Count Julian, 151–154, *151,* 161, 171

Ohio Company, 21
O'Neale, Jefferyes, *114*
optique (instrument), *144*

Palladian architecture, 10, *46*

at Mount Vernon, 155, *161*
  at Shirley Plantation, 56
Palladio, Andrea, 10, 132
paneling, 9
  at Mount Vernon, *157*
  at Shirley Plantation, 52
  at Wilton, *75, 78*
parquet floors, 123
parties, 15, 25–29
Peale, Charles Willson, *36,* 155
Phyfe, Duncan, *79*
pianofortes, *75*
pianos, 121–123, *124*
piazza, on Mount Vernon, 151, 154, *154*
Piedmont (Virginia), *88*
Pierson, William, 9
pineapples, 46, *52, 53*
plantation houses, 7
plantations, *8,* 12–15
  gardens in, *36*
  Shirley Plantation, 9, 46–58, *46*
Plummer, William, *60, 65*
Pocahontas, 11
polygraph (writing instrument), 125, *135, 140, 149*
porcelain, *108–117*
  at Mount Vernon, *163*
Potomac River, 11, *11, 151,* 154
Powel, Mrs. Samuel, *163*

Queen Anne style
  of furniture, *21*
  looking glass in, *105*
  of silversmithing, *60*
Queensware (Wedgwood), *108*

Ramsden, Jesse, *141*
Randolph, Benjamin, *148*
Randolph, Martha Jefferson, 121, *123*
Randolph, Molly, 78–82

Randolph, Peyton, 73
Randolph, Thomas Mann, 121
Randolph, William, II, *75*
Randolph, William, III, 73, 79
  Wilton built by, *73,* 75–78, 82, 97
Randolph, Williams (several individuals), 73
Randolph family, 73–78
Rappahannock River, 11, *11,* 94
recreation, 14–15, *14*
Revolutionary War, *see* American Revolution
Richmond (Virginia), *12,* 13, 121
Rittenhouse, David, *145*
Robb family, *92*
Rochambeau, Jean Baptiste, Comte de, *110*
rococo style of silversmithing, *60, 63*
Rolfe, Sir John, 11
Roman architecture, 121, 129, *129,* 132, 135
rooms, 9

scientific instruments, *140–149*
Scott, Peter, *53, 84, 86*
servants, 123–124
serving dishes, *108–117*
Sèvres (porcelain), *108, 113*
Sheraton, Thomas, *84*
Shirley Plantation, 9, 46–58, *46, 52*
  "flying" staircase at, *49*
  furniture at, *53, 86*
  kitchen for, *56*
  river entrance to, *58*
  silver at, *64*
  Wedgwood stoneware at, *109*
silver, *60–71*
  at Monticello, *129*

in Shirley Plantation, *49*, 53
slaves, 12–13, 78
society
   of eighteenth-century Virginia, 7
   large families in, 78
   of plantations, 12–15
   Revolution and, 15
   tobacco in, 11
Spotswood, Alexander, 8
Staffordshire (England), *108*
stairways
   of Shirley Plantation, 49, *49*
   of Stratford Hall, 17
   of Wilton, *75*
stone, 8
stoneware, *108–117*
   at Mount Vernon, *163*
Stratford Hall, 9, 17–32, *17*, *25*
   bedroom in, *29*
   counting room in, *33*
   furniture at, *90–91*
   Great Hall of, *21*
   kitchen for, *33*
   nursery in, *31*
   silver at, *71*
Sulgrave Manor (England), *42*
Swan, Abraham, 11, *53*, 161

Tayloe, John, 10
telescopes, *143*
theodolite (surveying instrument), *141*
thermometers, *143*
tobacco, *10*, 11, 12, 15
Townsend, John, *82*
trees, 20
Tyler, John, 56
Tyler, Julia, 56

Vaughan, Samuel, *155*, 157, *163*

Virginia, University of, 121, 138
Virginia House, garden at, *42–43*

War of 1812, 53–54
Washington, Augustine, 161
Washington, Betty (Lewis), 94, 97, 102–105, *102*
Washington, George, 7, 13, 15
   in American Revolution, 163–167
   Chinese porcelain of, *117*
   death of, *171*
   fox hunting by, *15*
   furniture of, *85*
   garden of, *36*, *37*
   Kenmore and, 97, 102, 105
   Lee family and, 17, 31
   Mount Vernon built by, 7, 151–163, *151*
   as president, 167–171
   silver owned by, *61*, *63*
   at Wilton, 79, 82
Washington, Lawrence, 157, 161
Washington, Lund, 101, 163–167
Washington, Martha Custis, *154*, 163, *171*
Washington (D.C.), 171
Webster, Noah, 167
Wedgwood, Josiah, *108*, *109*
Westover, *13*
Willard, Simon, *75*, *92*
William and Mary style of silversmithing, *60*
Williamsburg (Virginia), 12, 135
   furniture made in, *105*
   Governor's Palace in, 8, *12*
Wilton, 9, 73–82, *73*
   clock in, *92*
   furniture at, *82*, *87*, *88*

office in, *79*
stairway of, *75*
Windsor furniture
   chairs, *167*
   in Stratford Hall, *33*
Wollaston, John, *53*, *75*, *94*, *102*
Wood, Samuel, *63*
wood
   early Virginia houses built of, 8
   in Shirley Plantation, *53*
   see also furniture
Worcester (porcelain), *108*, *113*, *163*
Wren, Sir Christopher, 8–10, *12*, 78

York River, 11, *11*